REBUILDING
EMPIRES

REBUILDING
EMPIRES

HOW BEST BUY AND OTHER RETAILERS ARE TRANSFORMING AND COMPETING IN THE DIGITAL AGE OF RETAILING

THOMAS LEE

palgrave
macmillan

REBUILDING EMPIRES
Copyright © Thomas Lee, 2014.

All rights reserved.

First published in 2014 by
PALGRAVE MACMILLAN® TRADE
in the United States—a division of St. Martin's Press LLC,
175 Fifth Avenue, New York, NY 10010.

Where this book is distributed in the UK, Europe and the rest of the world,
this is by Palgrave Macmillan, a division of Macmillan Publishers Limited,
registered in England, company number 785998, of Houndmills,
Basingstoke, Hampshire RG21 6XS.

Palgrave® and Macmillan® are registered trademarks in the United States,
the United Kingdom, Europe and other countries.

ISBN 978–1–137–27933–0

Library of Congress Cataloging-in-Publication Data is available from the
Library of Congress.

A catalogue record of the book is available from the British Library.

Design by Newgen Knowledge Works (P) Ltd., Chennai, India.

First edition: December 2014

10 9 8 7 6 5 4 3 2 1

Printed in the United States of America.

CONTENTS

INTRODUCTION

NOT ROCKET SCIENCE

IN APRIL 2011, BEST BUY CO. ISSUED AN UNUSUAL STATEMENT THAT said CEO Brian Dunn had resigned from the company.

That Dunn resigned was not the unusual part. I had been covering Best Buy, based in Richfield, Minnesota, for the *Star Tribune* in Minneapolis for only eight months, but it didn't take a genius to figure out that Dunn was on the hot seat.

With the economy still recovering from the Great Recession and Amazon and Apple growing in strength, the world's largest consumer electronics retail chain was in serious trouble. Dunn, a longtime Best Buy veteran, seemed powerless to respond. Investors suggested it was time for Dunn to go.

Normally, a company that fires its CEO would say the executive left to "pursue other opportunities" or "spend more time with family." Instead, Best Buy's statement only said there were no "operational differences" between Dunn and Best Buy.

I soon learned from sources that the board of directors was investigating Dunn amid allegations that he used company resources to carry on an affair with a female employee. Throughout his career, Dunn had gained a reputation as an aggressive, hard-partying salesman. Inside Best Buy, it was an open secret that Dunn was fond of women. Maybe too much so.

Founder Dick Schulze eventually relinquished his chairmanship and left Best Buy only to launch a high-stakes effort to take the company private. In the end, Schulze dropped his bid and rejoined Best Buy as chairman emeritus.

If you exclude the melodrama, Best Buy's situation wasn't particularly unique. Across the industry, big-box retail was under attack by forces seemingly beyond its control: migration of traffic from stores to online retailers like Amazon, the rapid commoditization of once high-margin goods like electronics, the slow recovery of the American economy following the worst financial crisis since the Great Depression of the 1930s.

Circuit City and Borders are gone. Sears and JCPenney look listless. Even historically well-run retailers like Wal-Mart Stores, Inc. and Target Corp. feel enormous pressure. Best Buy's problems just happened to be more messy and sensational.

Big-box retailing is perhaps one of America's greatest innovations. From Costco to Walmart, these chains overwhelmed independent stores with brute force by leveraging their size to offer consumers selection and prices that competitors could not match.

Best Buy was one of the most successful of these big-box retailers. From just one electronics store in St. Paul, Minnesota, Schulze built a global empire that generates more than $50 billion in annual sales.

But Best Buy's knack for reinvention and innovation had faded over the previous few years, and the company fell victim to its own hubris and a wayward culture that was unable to adapt to the most disruptive force the industry has ever witnessed: the Internet.

Innovative players like Amazon and Apple and new technologies like smartphones and tablets have pushed old-fashioned brick-and-mortar retailers to the brink of irrelevance. As consumers purchase more of their goods online, big-box retailers find it harder and harder to convince shoppers to visit their stores.

Traffic to big box is like blood to human beings: you can't survive without a constant, steady flow. Without a certain number of people walking through those doors, the business model that underpins big box simply crumbles. Without shoppers, big-box chains are left with thousands of giant, half-full warehouses. Suddenly, the very thing that made big box successful—space—seems more like an albatross than a benefit.

But contrary to the doomsday declarations emanating from Wall Street and armchair pundits, big box is not dead nor will it be for some time. If ever.

As history consistently demonstrates, companies that survive turmoil are usually the ones that manage to replace complacency and dysfunction with innovation and sound judgment.

Walmart, for instance, launched an in-store service that allows shoppers to convert their DVDs to the cloud, where they can access the content on any mobile device. Target is collaborating with Facebook to drive consumers to its stores with the help of mobile devices and digital coupons.

"I think there is nothing wrong with a big store," said Nadia Shouraboura, a former top executive at Amazon. "I think the big store format is a good thing; it just needs to run much more efficiently and it needs to run much, much better. I don't think that big boxes will be dead. I think they will be a place for customers to try and play and experiment with products and walk away with what they want."

Best Buy has emerged as the biggest surprise of all. Just a year or two ago, people predicted the retailer would soon file for bankruptcy.

Today, the company, under new CEO Hubert Joly, has revitalized itself. Joly, a turnaround specialist who had no previous retail experience, adopted a strategy that favors, at least for now, improvement over reinvention.

He has so far resisted closing stores. Amazon and Apple aside, Best Buy, he argues, doesn't face an existential problem as much as a basic retail problem: promoting effective customer service, creating a user-friendly website, ensuring shelves are full of the right product.

"It's not rocket science," Joly told me.

The CEO has also embraced newer innovations like year-round price matching, shipping goods from stores to online customers, and leasing space to Samsung and Microsoft to operate their own stores inside Best Buy locations.

"People used to say our space was a liability," Joly said. "Now it has become an asset."

Joly didn't know it at the time, but he just eloquently summed up the vision behind this book: how big box can embrace, not repudiate, its largeness in the age of digital retail.

The book is divided into two sections: Part I examines the history of big-box retail, specifically focusing on Best Buy and Target. Part II examines the strategies those companies are deploying to better compete in a fast-changing industry.

For my research, I spoke to former executives and employees at Best Buy and Target along with several consultants, retail executives, analysts, and academics. I interviewed Best Buy CEO Hubert Joly on the record, but quotes from the company's other executives were not for attribution. My interviews with Target chief marketing officer Jeff Jones and digital chief Casey Carl were on the record. I also relied heavily on my reporting at the *Star Tribune*, retail books, and biographies privately published by Schulze and Bruce Dayton, one of five brothers who helped create Target.

Writing a book is no small chore and I had a lot of help to make it happen: the *Star Tribune*, notably former executive editor Nancy Barnes and current business editor Todd Stone, Palgrave Macmillan editor Laurie Harting, and my agent John Willig. Best Buy and Target provided invaluable cooperation. Finally, special thanks to John and Bonnie Oslund, Justin Miller, Alyssa Delaney, Jenna Ross, Amy Koo, Kim Garretson, Amy Von Walter, Glen Stubbe, and family and friends for their advice and support.

Part I

THE PAST

CHAPTER 1

EVERYTHING MUST GO

DICK SCHULZE STARED AT THE RUINS OF HIS ELECTRONICS STORE.

The ceiling was completely gone. Piles of speakers, VCRs, turntables, and televisions were strewn about. Wires were down everywhere, coming perilously close to the pools of rainwater collecting on the floor.[1]

The day started off normally enough. Aside from a heavy early morning rainfall that struck Minneapolis–St. Paul International Airport, June 14, 1981 boasted typical pleasant summer weather for the Twin Cities: sunny, 75 degrees, and a slight wind.

Schulze, the founder of a small, local electronics chain called the Sound of Music, decided to take his wife Sandy and three children to their lake cottage a couple of hours north of St. Paul.

Around 3 p.m., the National Weather Service issued a tornado watch in the metropolitan area. Schulze grew worried about his stores. While tornados in Minnesota are not as frequent or severe as in Kansas and Oklahoma, Schulze knew a twister could quickly destroy everything in its path.

He started to load the van.

SCHULZE GREW UP IN ST. PAUL immediately following World
War II. These were the postwar boom years, a period of economic
prosperity when a growing number of Americans craved cars,
suburban houses, and television sets, and many eagerly opened
their growing wallets for these luxuries.

By the time Schulze had graduated high school in 1958, he
had already stocked shelves at the Red Owl, a local grocery chain,
and worked for Montgomery Ward, where he organized packages for the national department store's large distribution center
in St. Paul.

By then, Schulze had developed a real taste for retail. After
completing high school and a stint with the U.S. Air Force, Schulze
went to work for his father.

Warren Schulze sold electronic components to industrial
customers like Honeywell and 3M. Dick focused on the smaller
consumer electronics business, working with national vendors
to peddle the latest equipment to retailers throughout the Upper
Midwest.[2]

Consumer electronics started to take off in the 1960s, with
factory shipments more than doubling in the decade thanks to
new innovations like color television, stereo sound, and transistor
radios.

At the same time, Japanese electronics, like Sony's 7-inch reel-
to-reel audio recorder, entered the country. By 1967, Japan accounted for 76 percent of all radio receivers and the vast majority
of tape recorders imported by the United States.[3]

The younger Schulze met with clients throughout the area, ex-
tolling the benefits of pricey products like Sherwood amplifiers and

tuners, Shure Brothers microphones and phonograph cartridges, and Garrard record changers. He loved every minute of it.

IN 1966, 26-YEAR-OLD DICK SCHULZE and his business partner, an old high-school classmate named Gary Smoliak, cobbled together enough money from family and friends to open the first Sound of Music shop at the corner of Hamline Avenue and St. Clair Avenue in St. Paul. At first, the two young entrepreneurs wanted to name their store Sound of the Northwest. Schulze and Smoliak didn't want to use the word "electronics" because their two main competitors at the time did.[4]

Schulze and Smoliak devised a relatively straightforward business strategy: they would use records and sheet music to lure customers into the store and then try to sell them speakers and stereos.

The St. Paul store, along with a second site in Dinkeytown, Minneapolis, was located near schools like the University of Minnesota and Macalester College, where crowds of students eagerly sought the latest music by The Beatles, The Rolling Stones, Bob Dylan, and Pink Floyd.

"I bought my first stereo at the Sound of Music," said Shawn Doyle, a St. Paul high-school student at the time who eventually became director of operations at Best Buy. "It was all about record players and turntables and reel-to-reel recorders. It was just the beginning of the technology age."

Sales at Sound of Music soared, from $173,000 during the first partial year of operation to $1.3 million in 1967.[5]

Schulze eventually bought out his partner and with the help of a local stock offering, Sound of Music grew to seven stores by the late 1970s with an annual revenue of $4 million.[6]

Then disaster literally struck.

SCHULZE AND HIS FAMILY RACED ALONG THE HIGHWAY, anxiously listening to the radio as the National Weather Service upgraded the tornado to a warning.

On June 14, 1981, around 3:49 p.m., a tornado touched near 50th Street and France Avenue in Edina, a town southwest of the Twin Cities, and continued northeast to Roseville. Packing winds up to 160 miles per hour, the twister knocked down power lines, smashed windows, and tore roofs off houses and buildings.

Suddenly, a news bulletin sounded on the radio: the tornado struck a shopping mall in Roseville and destroyed several businesses, including a Sound of Music store.

Schulze's heart sank.

At the moment the tornado struck, store manager Dave Telschow was helping a customer who wanted to buy a stereo. Suddenly, the roof ripped off the building, blasting VCRs off the wall like ping pong balls. Telschow, the customer, and two sales clerks dove for cover.[7]

It was over in a minute. Miraculously, no one was hurt, but the store was wiped out.

"I was the highest-ranking person there but I was probably the least capable person there," said Brad Anderson, a Sound of Music employee and future CEO of Best Buy. "I didn't know anything about electric wiring, about how to keep the employees safe."[8]

Schulze soon arrived and tried to salvage the merchandise. There wasn't much to save. It was still raining and the water had damaged most of the equipment.

Worse yet, the store generated most of Sound of Music's revenue and the company didn't have business interruption insurance. Schulze estimated profits could drop as much as 20 percent that year, assuming there were profits to lose.[9]

Before the tornado, "we got some relief from our creditors, we got some time, we started to make a tiny little bit of money," Anderson said. "We weren't making much before that and now we've lost our biggest store. So we're in pretty desperate straits."

The obvious thing to do, Schulze thought, was to sell as much as they could at markdown prices so the company could at least recoup some of its losses.

However, there wasn't enough sellable merchandise left at the Roseville store to offer a complete sale. So Schulze decided to raid Sound of Music's warehouses and other stores for overstock merchandise—discontinued models, display products, out-of-box items—and throw a "tent sale" at the Roseville site, which was already drawing large crowds of people wanting to get a firsthand look at the tornado damage.

The company flooded newspapers, TV stations, and radios with ads: *Tornado sale! Two days only! Get your BEST BUY on turntables, VCRs, speakers, tuners! Credit available!*[10]

The result was sheer chaos. Cars jammed the parking lots as long lines of people from across the region waited to get inside the tent or apply for credit at a trailer the company had set up. Schulze's wife, Sandy, even brought stacks of pizza to feed hungry employees and customers.

The sale took on a life of its own. Customers just wanted to grab as much stuff as they could and did not seem to care about prices. Schulze made another run at his warehouses and stores to resupply the tent for a second day. Again, the retailer sold out.

By the time the sale was over, Sound of Music had grossed more sales in two days than all seven stores typically generated in over 48 hours.[11]

Though physically exhausted, Schulze's mind began to race. What had just happened? Could Sound of Music somehow replicate this experience every day?

Schulze started to think big. Given the huge crowds that flocked to the tent sale, with enough stores and merchandise, perhaps the company could grow its sales to $50 million in just a few years.

Schulze knew he had hit on something. He just didn't know what it was yet.

CHAPTER 2

CHEAP CHIC

AROUND THE SAME TIME DICK SCHULZE WAS CONCEIVING SOUND OF Music, American retail was rapidly transforming.

Prior to World War II, small specialty shops and large urban department stores like Macy's in New York City, Kauffman's in Pittsburgh, and Marshall Fields in Chicago dominated the landscape.

Thanks to laws designed to protect mom-and-pop stores, large retailers could not win significant volume discounts from manufacturers. And those vendors had enough clout to force retailers to charge whatever price they set on merchandise. If a retailer failed to offer the preset price, manufacturers would just stop selling goods to the store.

But after the war, families grew much larger (the Baby Boom generation) and to save consumers time, retailers in the 1950s began stocking a wider assortment of merchandise: clothes, food, household essentials, and appliances.

"Back then, shopping had always been such a fragmented experience to where customers had to go from store to store to store," said Carol Spieckerman, president of newmarketbuilders consulting firm and an expert on big-box retailing. "Specialty retailers really owned their niches. They could charge pretty much whatever they wanted. The idea of having a one-stop shop and to be able to get these great values was just mind-blowing; for consumers to buy so many different products under one roof."

Bigger selection meant bigger stores, and to build bigger stores, retailers needed more real estate, an asset more readily available outside cities. President Eisenhower's Federal Highway Act of 1956, initially intended to help the military transport troops and goods more easily across state lines in times of war, instead created a housing boom in the suburbs. Suddenly, people with cars could commute to work in the city from greater distances. In response to the new car culture, big-box retailers added free parking to their stores and opened seven days a week, including Sunday.

"One of the prerequisites for the big box was the car," historian and author Marc Levinson told National Public Radio in 2012. "Everybody had to have a car because the big box was sitting out in a parking lot somewhere. The big box made shopping into a family experience. Mom and dad and the kids all piled into the car, they went out to this big store, and they could spend several hours there because there was, by the standards of the day, an enormous amount of merchandise."[1]

At the same time, states began relaxing restrictions on volume pricing, which, combined with the big-box retail format, gave birth to the concept of discount retailing.

Today, big-box multibillion discounters like Walmart and Costco dominate American retail, but back in the 1950s discount retail was hardly intuitive. Back then, manufacturers and retailers didn't appreciate the benefits of sound inventory management. The practice of accurately matching supply with demand was more art than science. Factories often made more than retailers needed, which meant excess goods sat unsold in warehouses.

"The value of logistics really was not seen in the retail communities yet," said Shawn Doyle, the former Best Buy operations director. "In a growing company, it's hard for somebody to say, 'Hey, I'm going to go spend $4 million on a distribution center.' 'What? I can open seven stores for that.'"

Retailers often carried too little of a particular product and it was not unusual to see a store manager drive to a warehouse and load up his car with merchandise to replenish his store.

As Schulze eventually figured out the day the tornado wiped out his store, retailers could attract huge crowds by selling overstock product that was just gathering dust in a distribution center.

In 1953, an entrepreneur opened one of the country's first discount department stores in an abandoned textile mill in New England. Ann & Hope somewhat resembled a Turkish bazaar by including goods sold beneath the manufacturer's list price and merchandise from individual specialty retailers like drug stores or sporting goods chains.

The following year, discount stores accounted for 15 percent of total retail sales. In 1962, Walmart and Kmart debuted, officially ushering in the era of big-box discount retail.

But discount retail doesn't simply mean selling *everything* really cheap. Otherwise, how could retailers ever make a profit? After all, different products carry different prices.

According to Spieckerman, big-box discounters grew successful because the complexity of their deep assortments forced them to manage inventory better.

"The whole science of multicategory retail really kicked off with mass retail," Spieckerman said. "It wasn't just every single thing in the store was cheaper. It wasn't just about putting everything out there and having a free-for-all. It was about strategic merchandising and constantly tweaking presentations in order to change the way people behaved in those environments. They were figuring out what they could get more money for and what they could charge less for. The more categories you sold, the more you could experiment."

Retailers started to pay more attention to how they presented the product to the shopper. Factors like lighting, store layout, and special product displays influenced consumer decisions. More importantly, big-box retailers adjusted prices in sophisticated ways, lowering prices on some goods to drive people into the store where they would later purchase higher-priced products with better profit margins.

One group of businessmen carefully observing these events were five brothers who ran a well-respected department store in downtown Minneapolis.

THE DAYTON CO. WAS UNUSUAL not because it was run by siblings. In fact, many venerable department stores at the time boasted family ownership and management.

But what set Dayton apart was the approach chosen by Ken, Wally, Donald, Bruce, and Douglas Dayton to run the business founded by their grandfather George. Not content to live off a lucrative inheritance, the Dayton boys were determined to preserve familial peace by continuing to grow the business, whether through geography or, perhaps more crucially, format.

"Though they managed well together, one department store was not big enough for five of them," Bruce Dayton said. "For both financial and take-charge reasons, they wanted to make a bigger pie, perhaps several pies. Working together on a broader, deeper playing field, they could make the most of the opportunity their father had provided."[2]

"Next, the brothers decided, they were paying too high a price for harmony, for not rocking the boat," Dayton continued. "They decided that profit, not harmony, would be the goal. Profit would produce family harmony in the long run; conversely, a lack of profit would produce disharmony among the families. Profit would be the goal; it would fuel their growth. And their business must do both—produce profit and grow—at the same time."[3]

By the early 1950s, Dayton's was the dominant retailer in the Twin Cities but the brothers felt the department store was starting to lose its sway over the consumer. As retailers started to expand beyond their traditional home markets, the family also feared out-of-town competitors would soon come to Minneapolis and St. Paul.

The brothers consulted with a real estate expert who was working on the country's first shopping center near Seattle for Detroit-based department store chain J. L. Hudson's. The expert convinced Dayton's to do something similar in the fast-growing suburbs of the Twin Cities.

Dayton's ultimately paid $3 million to buy 500 acres in what is today the upscale suburb of Edina, about seven miles from Minneapolis. In place of the existing cornfield, the brothers ultimately envisioned an 800,000-square-foot shopping center with the usual comforts of a modern mall, including multiple department store anchors (Dayton's and rival L. S. Donaldson & Co.), over 70 specialty shops, a grocery store, escalators, a courtyard, and lots of free parking.[4]

But what really made Southdale Center special was its distinction as the country's first enclosed, fully air-conditioned mall, which made shopping a 365-day-a-year reality in a state known for its cold, long winters. The mall, which officially opened in 1956, featured an innovative climate control system that kept the temperature at a constant 75 degrees. It would heat the building during the winter using water it had stored and warmed in the summer. Southdale would pipe in music during the day and detect sound at night to protect the mall from thieves and intruders. A tunnel and elevators allowed for underground deliveries.

Southdale offered an appealing alternative to shoppers wary of the traffic in the restricted space of downtown Minneapolis.

"You would go to Edina because of the parking," said Gary Zawoski, a longtime Twin Cities shopper. "It was a major convenience. You go as a family or a group of guys with their girlfriends. You go to a movie. There was always that variety. You park in one place and all of sudden you've spent a couple of hours there. You got everything you wanted under one roof, which was especially useful because six of the twelve months out of the year in Minnesota is bad weather. If you were a low-income person but your kids had higher tastes you went to Southdale to be exposed to something unique and special. It was a step up."

The company's experience with suburban mall development allowed it to pursue another innovative store format: the discount store.

In 1960, a gentleman by the name of Ira Hayes spoke to the Dayton brothers at their monthly management meeting. Hayes represented the National Cash Register Co. (today called NCR Corp.) but he wasn't in town to sell more cash registers to the Daytons.

Instead, he excitedly told the brothers of discount stores he had seen in the old textile mills of New England: long lines of customers with carts piled high with bargain-priced clothing waiting patiently for the next available checkout counter. The free-for-all atmosphere was a far cry from the refined, elegant environment the Daytons cultivated at their department stores.

The discount format may have lacked elegance but selling a broader assortment of regularly discounted merchandise to a broader group of customers offered a potential market greater than any department store could ever hope to muster. Sure, retailers would lose money on some discounted items but the increased traffic would more than compensate those losses, or as Hayes said: "islands of loss among seas of profit."[5]

Hayes told the Daytons of a conversation he had with a skeptical merchandiser from England.

"Sir, do you realize that the Queen of England shops at our store?" the man said. "What will she think of standing in a checkout line?"

"But how many Queens do you have?" Hayes shot back.

The Daytons knew discount retailing was coming to the Twin Cities whether they liked it or not, so they best strike first.

Nevertheless, discount was an entirely different breed of retail animal than department stores. For one thing, discount stores would have to offer consistently low prices every day. Department stores, by contrast, used infrequent special sales to draw customers. Discount stores also operated at a much lower profit margin than department stores' normal 40 percent. That means discounters' profits depended as much (if not more) on controlling costs through supply chain efficiencies and leveraging economics of scale than simply selling more products.

The company visited several discount stores in the East but dismissed most of them as "schlock." No, if the retailer wanted to pursue a discount format, the company would do it its own way.

In 1962, the same year Walmart and Kmart opened their doors, the brothers opened four discount stores in Minnesota that they called Target. Although the Daytons insisted on operating their discount and department stores as independent business units, Target was heavily influenced by its department store roots.

About 40 percent of the 100,000 or so items Target carried were identical to products sold at the downtown Minneapolis department store.[6] The company also found the same customers were shopping at both Dayton's and Target.

That consumers would confuse Target with Dayton's was not a surprise, Zawoski, the Twin Cities shopper, said. The retailer's original downtown department store featured a basement where consumers could find markdown prices. Every now and then, the retailer would stock a few of its shelves with basement merchandise at a regular department store price, he recalled. But once a customer decided to buy the product, the company would charge the basement price to give the shopper the illusion of finding a great bargain.

"The typical person did not know what a discount store was," Zawoski said. "You've got to remember there were only five places you could shop in the Twin Cities. There were no discount prices unless it went on sale."

At first, Target performed poorly. The company struggled to clear about $1 million worth of overstock products, mostly because the retailer did not adequately monitor its inventory.[7] Customer returns were high.

But the brothers also saw some positive signs. Customers who returned merchandise didn't simply walk out of the store after they received their cash. For every $30 Target would refund to its customers, shoppers spent $20 on other goods during the same trip.[8]

Eventually, Target adjusted its merchandise mix and adopted an IBM computer to keep track of inventory. By 1965, the chain generated a 25 percent return on assets. Target's new store in Bloomington hit its goal of $10 million in sales.[9]

More importantly, Target had started to establish a distinct identity from its discount competitors. While Walmart focused on selling everyday household goods to customers in rural regions and small towns, Target adhered to the upscale, urban department store customer that defined Dayton's. At the same time, Target's operational independence from Dayton's allowed both chains to make decisions that best fit their format.

Other department stores like Woolworth's and Federated tried to roll out discount spinoffs but those formats struggled to forge a distinct identity from the core business. Dayton's and Target made sure to keep their two operations apart.[10] The two chains operated separate mainframe computers and fought to keep each other's merchandise from landing on the other's shelves.

Yet Dayton's upscale department store sensibilities, including the retailer's penchant for cost control, experimentation, and fashion-forward urgency, continued to influence Target's merchandising strategy.

"While it had no price tag, Dayton's merchandisers were well aware of how fashion came and went," Bruce Dayton said. "They used a merchandising curve to test and determine how much to order and when to stop ordering a particular fashion, so that they could achieve maximum sales with no overstock. The concept and its practice (having managers think about the curve) made everyone more fashion-conscious and thus improved merchandising, increased sales, and decreased out-of-date inventory."[11]

In the late 1960s, in a bid to expand beyond traditional female customers, the Dayton's store on Nicollet Mall in downtown Minneapolis hosted "College Night," which brought 8,000 students for a ticketed four-floor event outside of regular business hours. Today, Target hosts similar college shopping parties at midnight around the Back to School week, hiring buses to ferry students from and to campuses. The Dayton's store also featured "Young Idea Center," which offered advice to 18- to 35-year-olds on home furnishings, color coordination, window treatments, and room arrangement.

In many ways, the retailer's focus on youth, design, and limited inventory helped produced Target's most prominent innovation: the limited edition design partnerships.

Today we take for granted that Target will launch a design collection that will prompt people to line up outside stores for the first crack at the merchandise. But 40 years ago, the idea that a discount chain could work with an upscale designer to create clothing and housewares for the mass consumers was not only laughable but also sacrilegious to the elite fashion world.

"In the early years, Target couldn't get the hot brand names," journalist Laura Rowley wrote in *On Target*. "Mass was crass: Companies keep their goods out of discounters to protect their elite images, and those who dared to traverse the line suffered."[12]

"In 1982, the fashion designer Halston—the icon known for the pillbox hat worn by Jackie Kennedy in the 1960s and the slinky look of Studio 54 in the 1970s—created an affordable collection for JCPenney," she wrote. "The move devastated Halston's couture business, as Bergdorf Goodman and other stores promptly dropped the line."[13]

Even the feds took offense at the prospect of a mass/luxury marriage. In 1979, the Federal Bureau of Investigation probed Target's acquisition of 21,000 pairs of Calvin Klein, Gloria Vanderbilt, and Sassoon jeans.

"Target widely advertised its coup: 'These are the same jeans sold for $35 elsewhere, not discounter styles or close out. When they're gone there will be no more,'" Rowley wrote. "The jeans reportedly sold out within hours at some stores and within a week across the entire 80-store chain. Klein, Vanderbilt, and Sassoon contacted federal authorities and sued Target, saying the goods must have been stolen."[14]

After Target produced evidence that it had indeed bought the goods from a wholesaler, the FBI dropped the case.

But Target felt it was onto something. Clearly, there was a huge demand for luxury goods at discount prices.

"Every brand has aspirational consumers, people who want to do a little better," said Steve Dennis, a retail consultant and former chief strategy officer for luxury goods chain Neiman Marcus. "What Target really understood is that just because you're a cash-constrained consumer, doesn't mean you don't aspire to have more design sensibility. You can still go after the Walmart on price but also push the envelope on how to trade up a little bit."

But where could the retailer get that higher-scale merchandise? The solution: create its own "luxury" products.

In 1999, Target launched a collection of home goods designed by architect Michael Graves, which included kitchen gadgets, utensils, and even placemats. The partnership was a huge hit, even though Graves was not a household name at the time.

But Target figured out a winning formula, Dennis said. "Some of Target's early partnerships were not with well-known designers, but what they had was real credibility. Michael Graves was known to a very small number of people, but he had a story that Target could build a brand around. Target built awareness but not completely from scratch. Target found people who had real stories and credibility."

Eventually, Target became the go-to retailer for luxury brands that had lost favor with consumers as well as promising young designers looking for exposure.

"As time went on, Target took on brands that were kind of in decline with the core customer," Dennis said. "Missoni, for example, was a luxury brand but basically died. I bet you that if you asked someone to name 20 great designers, nobody would come up with Missoni. But Target made it cool to their customers."

WITH THE SUCCESS OF THE TORNADO sale still fresh in his mind, Dick Schulze grew bullish. Suddenly, Sound of Music, with each of its ten stores approximately the size of a local coffee shop, seemed too small for Schulze's ambitions. He wanted to get big. Very big.

"I remember coming into town for my interview," said Al Lenzmeier, Best Buy's former chief operating officer and vice chairman. "Dick Schulze pulled out a spreadsheet on accounting paper. He showed me his plan of going from $25 million in sales at the time to $500 million—in just five years. I thought: 'That guy is goofy.' You get a one-in-a-million chance to participate in something like that."[15]

Given the growing dominance of discount electronics superstores like Circuit City on the East Coast and Highland Superstores in Detroit, Schulze felt the Twin Cities market was ripe for such a format. And with his experience and connections with manufacturers, he was the man to do it.

First, Schulze needed a new name. He wanted his company to sell a lot more product beyond records and posters, so Sound of Music wasn't going to cut it anymore. Schulze remembered the phrase "Best Buy" from the ad he bought for the tornado sale.

Schulze wanted to avoid competing with bigger chains on price alone. Instead, the company would sell consumers on the concept of value and assortment. Best Buy would not just sell stereos but also computers, cameras, and washing machines.

Schulze decided to build a 25,000-square-foot big box in Burnsville, a suburb south of the Twin Cities, just off Highway 13, the main east-west road at the time. He wanted to capture the same vibrancy of the tornado sale along with the wide assortment of electronics found at the larger discount chains.

The Best Buy store in Burnsville officially opened its doors on Saturday, October 1, 1983, and had revenue over $14 million in the first year. This was higher than the rest of the Sound of Music stores combined. Over the next five years, Best Buy quickly grew across the Twin Cities and then the rest of the Midwest.

"The strategy was to build out in concentric circles," Lenzmeier said. "The metro, out-state, Iowa, Wisconsin, North Dakota."

Inside the stores, an aggressive, ego-driven boys' culture dominated the sales floor. Best Buy store employees, known as Blue Shirts, earned a certain percentage of the profit margin the retailer generated from individual products like camcorders, televisions, and VCRs. In addition, vendors often paid salesmen $50 "bonuses" to push their merchandise.

While retail today offers relatively low wages, a Blue Shirt in 1985 could make $35,000 a year in commissions, or about

$76,000 in today's dollars, said Matt Henderson, who worked at two Best Buy stores during that period.

"This was a really crazy time," Henderson said. "You would literally stand there and you have your order pad. People would line up all day long. You could make a couple of thousand commissions in one day. That's a lot of money. The shelves were empty and people would still buy whatever."

But Best Buy's biggest moneymaker wasn't even a physical product. The company required the Blue Shirts to aggressively peddle warranties, or extended service protection plans, especially on high-end VCRs.

"You could be selling lots of product and have good margin but you would still be in trouble if you did not have 8 percent of your sales in warranties," Henderson said. "You would keep the VCR top open and the whole time you are trying to set customers up to buy a warranty, try to tell them all of the things that go wrong. Here's all the maintenance work you have to do. Get your VCR cleaned up."

"You try to sell them a two-year warranty for $80 on a VCR they spent $200, $300 on," he continued. "You could sell a lot of product but you could be out of the door if you didn't sell warranties. They really, really pushed that. You tried to scare the customer but you do it subtly enough. You want to let them know that it's a good product but not good enough that you don't need this warranty."

To keep their Blue Shirts motivated, the company regularly published individual sales numbers, something akin to a scene out of *Glengarry Glen Ross*. Beat your sales goals and be treated like a rock star. Miss them and be shamed out the door.

"During the day, one of the store managers would get on an internal loudspeaker and the call would go out," said a former advertising executive and Blue Shirt. "Ostensibly, it was a supposedly innocuous call for a clerk to call an extension number such as 695. The reality was the extension number was actually the clerk's sales figure. 6.95 percent of the store's sales. Everyone could measure each other."[16]

Things got so competitive that store managers would frequently raid a warehouse for hot products, leaving nothing for other stores. Again, inventory management was in name only. It was every store for itself.

"Best Buy would have a big sale, and this thing was going on sale on Sunday," Doyle said. "One of the ambitious little store managers would know it was coming up and he's ordering all of them in the distribution center to ship to his store because he was going to make all his revenue."

"We knew that there was some hoarding going on," he said. "The culture was such that sell, sell, sell, sell, sell, and if you're going to have an item that's going to be hot that's going to sell, I want to have as much of it as I can get."

Most of the Blue Shirts were single men in their twenties who suddenly were earning thousands of dollars in commissions a day. They also enjoyed generous discounts on the latest pricey electronics. After the stores closed, the Blue Shirts often went to the bar at Stuart Anderson Cattle Co. restaurant off I-394 to brag about their sales takes. Employees would also throw wild apartment parties with generous amounts of booze and cocaine.

"Everybody had money," Henderson said. "It was a great time to be working in retail. You had the best electronics gear bought for cheap. You had the best stereo in your car. You had the best video, audio in the house. You had all of these toys. It was fun. It was like a big frat house in some ways. A lot of employees were cavorting with each other that way. I didn't want to say it was drugs, sex, and rock 'n' roll, but it was whatever Minnesota was doing that was closest to that thing."

But the good times would not last long. As Best Buy grew in sales and stature, one national chain was not about to let Best Buy usurp its position as the top electronics retailer in the Midwest.

With 50-plus stores and annual revenue of $656 million, Highland was the first out-of-town competitor to directly challenge Best Buy. Highland's modus operandi was to open stores sometimes literally across the street from its rivals and use its clout with suppliers to launch a price war the rivals could not hope to win.

Sure enough, Highland entered the Twin Cities in May 1986 with three superstores in Minnetonka, West St. Paul, and Brooklyn Center—yes, all close to Best Buy stores and, in the case of Brooklyn Center, adjacent to the Best Buy location.

Best Buy prepared the best they could. The company tried to hold down costs. At the same time, it spent lavishly on growth: the company expanded some of its stores to between 25,000 to 40,000 square feet. Best Buy also opened stores in Milwaukee, a preemptive strike against Highland's plans for Wisconsin.

But the real battle was in the Twin Cities stores, with each chain trying to undercut the other's prices. Every day, Best Buy and Highland employees scoped out each store's deals and adjusted their own prices accordingly.

"That was a very unfun time to work for Best Buy," Henderson said. "Highland put a store across the street from Minnetonka. All of a sudden, there was competition. We go into these other stores, we literally walked through to see what they were selling and for how much and they would do the same thing. We had someone follow them and tail them all of the time. It was back and forth like this every day."

The price cuts "lowered our commissions," he said. "I had to sell more product. Everyone took a hit on how much they were making when Highland came into town. It got so competitive that I don't think there was enough margin left to make any money. Before Highland came in, [pay] was extremely lucrative. Highland really cramped everything when they came in. It was a retail war. When there's war, it's no fun to be a private. They're out to take the other store out."

Other electronics chains jumped into the fray.

Doyle recalls an incident when a tornado (yes, another tornado) destroyed a Highland distribution center in Texas. Banks Electronics, another retailer based in Dallas, bought all of the leftover inventory and attempted to sell the products in the Twin Cities. Dick Schulze would have none of that.

"Dick said, 'Okay, anybody who has a trailer or truck or whatever, you go to Banks and buy everything you can,'" Doyle said. "'You write a check and we'll have a [reimbursement] check for you in your hands the next day before your check clears.' All of this stuff came back into our warehouse. Dick didn't want people here to buy this stuff lower than what we were selling at."

Ironically, Best Buy sold Highland's own inventory at prices much lower than Highland could offer.

"It was a street fighter thing that we had in us," Lenzmeier said.

The price war took a toll on both companies. Saddled with debt and overexpansion, Highland closed its Twin Cities stores in 1991.

Best Buy crowed about its victory and the normally frugal Schulze even threw a lavish, black-tie party at the Hyatt Regency ballroom in downtown Minneapolis to celebrate Highland's retreat.

"I was there the day that Highland announced they were closing," Doyle said. "That was one of the highest points of the whole thing. Highland is out of business, and we just rejoiced. We have slain the monster, and we did the same to Silo Electronics and Electronics Universe. Everything kept clicking."

But in truth, Best Buy took a severe beating. The company's sales jumped significantly during its war with Highland, but its profits nearly evaporated, hitting a low of $2.1 million in 1989.

By his own admission, Schulze was not a great business thinker or strategist. He had never gone to college or worked for a big corporation. But Schulze was a tenacious salesman and hardboiled entrepreneur who did not shy away from a fight.

Above all else, Schulze possessed a supernatural talent to improvise, to stave off disaster (and bankruptcy) even when failure was all but certain. He seemed to thrive best in a crisis, when his optimism and steely will won over even the most ardent of doubters.

Yet Schulze's best traits often worked against him, especially when there was no crisis to conquer. Best Buy was mostly built on improvisation, luck, and guts, but large corporations can't survive on those qualities alone.

"We'd been operating in a 'cowboy culture,'" Brad Anderson, a former CEO, said. "It was 'anything goes' if it works. We believed in people and there were numbers they were supposed to hit and they had enormous freedom to do it. But the problem was we were selling great, but there was chaos with our inventory and we couldn't make enough money. Dick was not curious about this."

Low on cash, Schulze offered to sell Best Buy to Circuit City in 1988 for $30 million in cash and stock. CEO Rick Sharp ultimately declined, partly because Schulze would own a significant chunk of Circuit City stock and command a role on the board of directors.

"At the time, Sharp's view was that it was not necessary to spend $30 million when all Circuit City had to do was open one store in Minneapolis and 'blow them away,'" former Circuit City chairman and CEO Alan Wurtzel wrote in his book *Good to Great to Gone*. "In hindsight, had Circuit City acquired Best Buy for $30 million in stock and cash, it would have been the best money we ever spent. At least it would have eliminated a future competitor."[17]

In truth, consumer electronics retailers at this time were dropping like flies, the result of bankruptcies, liquidations, and consolidation: Silo (1985), Newmark and Lewis (1992), Highland (1993), Luskins (1997), and Lechmere (1997), to name a few.

As it turned out, Best Buy's war with Highland was only a microcosm of the industry's larger problems. Consumer electronics were fast becoming commodities and several retailers suffered from a toxic combination of debt-fueled overexpansion and profit-draining price wars.

For Best Buy to survive, the company would need to offer something else to the consumer other than sales gimmicks and endless price cuts.

CHAPTER 3

THE BURNING PLATFORM

WHAT THE HECK IS GOING ON OVER THERE?

In 1986, as Best Buy and Highland escalated their bloody price war, Dick Schulze was driving down I-494 when he noticed commotion outside a Sam's Club, the wholesale deep discount chain operated by Walmart.

Cars circled the lot, searching vainly for a parking spot to open up. Happy customers left the store with a bounce in their step, carts piled high with groceries, clothing, and consumer electronics. Schulze had seen that look before, five years ago at Sound of Music's tornado sale in Roseville.

The Sam's Club store couldn't have been more different than Best Buy or Highland. Instead of slick salespeople aggressively stalking customers, the enormous store was stacked high with every imaginable product and shoppers just grabbed whatever they wanted.

As Schulze drove home, he knew that the retail world was rapidly changing. Even if Best Buy fended off Highland, he would eventually face off against Circuit City, Sam's Club, and Wal-mart.

Schulze made a fateful decision. Perhaps the best way to beat Highland or any other national competitor wasn't to compete completely on price or assortment but rather to empower customers to make their own decisions. Instead of hawking a VCR or extended warranty plan the customer may or may not have needed, Best Buy would empty its inventory onto the sales floor and let the shopper go nuts. The Blue Shirts would still be around but in a "facilitator" role, ready to dispense help only when customers asked.

"There were a lot of products that were new," former employee Matt Henderson said. "People were always getting their first VCR or first stereo so Best Buy did a lot of internal product training. You got to act and feel like you're a professional. You got to really learn the equipment and be an expert. When people got in the store, you had good prices but you had answers. I took a lot of pride in my work. They had full-time people making sure employees knew the products they were selling."

But to make sure Blue Shirts would best serve the customers' needs, Best Buy needed to scrap the commission-based pay system that had long dominated the consumer electronics business. Up until this point, salesmen would boost their income by selling as many products and warranties as they could, regardless of whether or not the customers needed them. Vendors would also throw in a few extra bucks called "spiffs" if a salesman would nudge customers toward their merchandise.

"It felt like a big Ponzi scheme," said a former ad executive and Blue Shirt. "Manufacturers are giving bonuses to the stores for selling a product. The store is selling the product by having the salesperson push the product and the warranties. It was bonus, bonus, bonus. And it was sketchy, in my mind."

Under Schulze's new system, Best Buy would directly pay its managers and Blue Shirts set salaries. Eliminating commissions would lower employee pay but it would also remove the temptation of greasing sales for personal financial gain. For the first time, a big-box discounter would distinguish itself not by undercutting the competition, but rather by the ability of its employees to offer expert, neutral advice to shoppers.

In other words, Best Buy would win on service and experience, not price. The Blue Shirts, not size or sales gimmickry, became the company's secret sauce.

IN MANY WAYS, FORMER CEO BRAD ANDERSON was always an outlier at Best Buy, a rather restless man more comfortable with management theory and reading books on Napoleon than partying with the Blue Shirts after the work day ended.

His path to Best Buy CEO was a highly unlikely one. Born in Sheriden, Wyoming, Anderson moved to the Twin Cities when he was six and eventually attended the University of Denver, where he studied sociology and history. After graduating, Anderson, the son of a Lutheran pastor, returned to Minnesota and enrolled at Northwestern Lutheran Theological Seminary in St. Paul. He dropped out after one year.

One day Anderson walked into a Sound of Music store in West St. Paul to purchase a stereo. A big music fan, Anderson wound up joining the store as a salesman.

He was pretty awful: Anderson failed to make a single equipment sale during his first two weeks. His first paycheck netted him a grand total of $69 for 120 hours of work.

Anderson thought about quitting but decided to stick it out. He eventually became a store manager. But he grew antsy again.

"I'd spent seven years being bored out of my mind running a store," Anderson said.[1]

Over the next 20 years, Schulze and Anderson formed a close, if volatile, partnership. They often bitterly argued but always found a way to move forward.

"You'd think Brad was going to get fired the way they went at it," said George Lapouch, a former vice president of strategy at Best Buy. "But during breaks they'd pat each other on the back, be talking about baseball scores."[2]

When Schulze decided to step down as CEO, he chose Anderson to replace him. Not because they agreed on strategy or even because Schulze thought Anderson commanded great business acumen. Schulze felt Anderson's penchant for hard work and loyalty best embodied Best Buy's culture.

However, Anderson and Schulze clashed often, mostly because of their different temperaments and styles. Schulze was the gritty entrepreneur who followed his instincts; Anderson established a reputation as an intellectual, enamored with strategy, consultants, and modern management concepts.

"Brad had the vision of wanting to understand how big leaders led successful companies," Shawn Doyle, the former operations director, said. "Dick was an entrepreneur and just said, 'We're going to go this way.' Then everybody followed and we just did."

Anderson, however, believed in consensus, building broad-based support before Best Buy made any big decision. To some, Anderson was a thoughtful, strategic leader who listened to outside experts and employees, especially the Blue Shirts.

"Dick's an eternal optimist," Al Lenzmeier said. "He'd talk about how he slept through the night without a worry. Brad and I would be the ones who'd lose sleep worrying about the company."[3]

For example, in 1997, the company generated nearly $8 billion in annual revenue but only $1.2 million in profit, a margin of less than 1 percent. Anderson pushed to hire an outside consulting firm to rework Best Buy's supply chain but Schulze initially resisted. He had insisted that Best Buy had a "world class" inventory system.

In reality, it was a mess. The stores carried only 75 percent of the product they were supposed to carry; Schulze thought the number was actually 90 percent.

"Dick was in denial," said Robert Willett, one of the consultants the company had hired who later joined Best Buy's senior leadership team as chief information officer and international head. "He is a very proud man."

At the same time, he also was easily swayed by senior leaders who offered a rosier picture than the actual situation, Willett said. "He blew with the wind. If you were the last one to leave the office, you would be the last person he listened to."

BY 2002, BEST BUY WAS IN GOOD SHAPE: sales were strong and profits soared, as did the stock price. But Anderson saw only disaster ahead.

"We were on fire but you had to look at the horizon," Anderson said. "You knew the world of retailing. But you knew you couldn't just sell hardware in the future. Too many people in the company didn't see it out there. The burning platform far on the horizon. I was terrified by it... I don't know what I'm selling tomorrow."[4]

Up to this point, Best Buy thrived on selling the latest technology (VCRs, stereos, computers) to gadget-hungry customers. But the time between a high-priced new product introduction to a low-priced commodity was quickly shrinking. And more competitors like Walmart and Target were expanding into consumer electronics. Under Schulze, Best Buy's response had been to train and incentivize a skilled sales force and rework its inventory systems. But Best Buy's business model was hardly unique.

"Mass retail has been so influential on retail as a whole and it's not like they got to keep all of the supply chain efficiencies to themselves," Carol Spieckerman of newmarketbuilders said. "A lot of these [mass retail people] had migrated to other retailers to help them. There's been a lot of cross-pollination of talent that has allowed other retailers to realize those same types of efficiencies. They're certainly not proprietary. I think retail as a whole has benefited from mass retail."

Anderson and Schulze fought over what to do: Should Best Buy radically change or stick to tradition and ride out the storms like it had always done?

"We just thought the path was very different," Anderson said. "We just completely didn't agree on how to get there. To me, there was only one option. Strategically, we had to go deeper on what our customers' needs were. We had to have a different lens. What's the direction of the customer? That's the Genesis point."[5]

Schulze "looked to those he trusted most," Anderson continued. "The kinds of people who showed up at the tent sale and salvaged the equipment from the tornado. The kids, the folks who worked the aisles. Follow the Blue Shirts. Help them figure it out and articulate it."[6]

Much to the shock of Best Buy veterans used to Dick Schulze's dominating presence at corporate headquarters, Anderson inaugurated his reign by heading off to Yale University for several months—to think.

"I had a question: Where is the world moving?" Anderson said. "It was a highly contentious decision seen from the inside. Because it looks like a dereliction of duty on my part. That I should be back running it just as Dick had."[7]

By 2002 the digital age had arrived, and with it a new era of low-cost technology available to all. While a computer might have seemed a curious luxury in the 1980s, families now regularly own multiple PCs in their homes. Websites like Yahoo! and eBay, not hardware, dominated the public's imagination. Instead of buying CDs and tapes, consumers now cherry picked music from the Internet.

Despite its success, Best Buy throughout its history had stumbled from one existential crisis to another, relying more on improvisation, will power, and plain luck to survive. Anderson wanted to break that cycle: for once, Best Buy would anticipate industry shifts and not simply react to them.

"I went to Yale to look for options for Best Buy that I could not see from within the boundaries of the company," Anderson said. "The company had already almost gone out of business at least twice when it was late in adapting to societal change that impacted our industry. When you looked at the impact of digital technology on people's lives, it seemed substantially bigger and faster than historical forces of the Industrial Age. With greater change on the horizon, I had to use the time before taking over as CEO to the best possible use. In my opinion, most leaders only get one shot at transformational change and that is right when they start. So I had better get this right if I was to make a contribution as a CEO."[8]

Anderson ultimately created a strategy that seemed like a natural evolution from Schulze's ideas on customer service during Best Buy's war with Highland in the late 1980s. Back then, Best Buy needed to give customers something more than just slashed prices. The company had already trained its Blue Shirts to offer expert advice to shoppers, and Schulze had scrapped the commission-based system to ensure they also gave unbiased advice.

Anderson would take it one or even two steps forward. Best Buy would deepen its expertise in technology to the point that customers would pay something extra for such service. But perhaps more radically, the Blue Shirts would not just simply sell products but rather *offer solutions* to customers' needs that might involve selling them *several* products at once.

As a result, the Blue Shirts would need to act as de facto anthropologists, breaking down their customers into defined lifestyle segments around which Best Buy could build its merchandise, service, and even store designs. With that kind of intelligence, Best Buy would always be on top, if not ahead, of emerging consumer trends.

"Do you think innovation is going to come from some people looking at data sheets at the office?" Anderson said. "Or do you think that the innovation is going to come organically from your customer touch points?"[9]

Corporate headquarters was far too removed from the things store employees experienced every day. Who better but Blue Shirts to figure out what customers want or need? Anderson's ideas later evolved into a concept called "Customer Centricity."

"For me the evidence is overwhelming," he said. "If you go back to the roots of the things that Best Buy does that work, you will find that root over and over again. And you will almost never find some corporate executive poring over [data] because you're isolated from the direct customer experience that the Blue Shirt guy's got."[10]

Anderson's first major move as CEO was to purchase Geek Squad. Founded in 1994, the Minneapolis-based firm specialized in on-site and remote computer repair services. Under Best Buy, Geek Squad morphed into a global brand of its own; the unit today generates about $2 billion a year, or about 4 percent of Best Buy's annual revenue.

But back in 2002, Best Buy perhaps did not realize the true potential of Geek Squad, said former chief information officer Willett. Aside from a cult following, the firm was little known outside of the Twin Cities. Best Buy bought Geek Squad, which was losing money, for a modest price.

At the time, the idea of 24-hour PC tech support seemed quixotic at best.

"In those particular years, there wasn't a great deal of PC support," Willett said. "It was sort of, buy a computer and take your chances. We really didn't have a long-term strategy. We were just trying to get into the repair business."

But over time, Geek Squad not only became a lucrative source of revenue but also a way for the retailer to establish a long-term relationship with customers that lasted well after they left the store. Instead of just selling PCs, Best Buy could charge flat service fees to repair, upgrade, and maintain the product until consumers bought a new computer.

"When you look at the complete product cycle, we wanted to control more of the circle," Willett said. "Service was a natural extension. It wasn't transactional. In the past, you were only as good as the stores' take for the day. Selling services for 24 hours a day, 365 days a year meant we can make money while we were asleep."

With their trademark white shirts and skinny black ties, Geek Squad agents would also nicely complement Blue Shirts in providing expert advice on products, a value-added service that could distinguish Best Buy from its big-box competitors.

"Geek Squad had the same values as Best Buy," Willett said. "Put the two together and it was off to the races."

"We acquired Best Buy Corporation because I couldn't do this alone," Geek Squad founder Robert Stephens joked at a tech conference in 2008. "We've been working with them for a long time and I thought, 'now there's a mammoth challenge.' They need the service help, we all know that. But their number-one priority is the product. Let's combine the two great tastes. You know it's easy to offer a great experience when you're a small company like Geek Squad. Now try and do it to a $25 billion organization."

"When we joined forces with Best Buy, I said, 'Listen, we have 4,000 kids behind those service counters. Those kids are fine, they're actually much better at service than they were allowed to be.' If we can take the handcuffs off them, give them a costume, and tell them what their role is in saving the world, by saving your hard drives, and frame it up that way, they'll feel better about their jobs."[11]

Stephens first established his reputation as a computer Mr. Fix-It while working at the University of Minnesota's Human Factors Research Lab in the early 1990s.

"During this time, some titanic social shifts occurred," Stephens said. "A little company called America Online decided to bet on a strategy of mailing a disc to every American three times a week. Electronic stores that sold TVs and appliances were starting to sell computers and marketed to average people."[12]

"When I was working at the research lab, I saw the Internet, the web browser, and remember installing the first version of Linux," he continued. "Because university research jobs don't pay very well, I was making money on the side riding my mountain bike around Minneapolis fixing computers for people. Remember in the early 90s, you couldn't even open up *Newsweek* or turn on the television without hearing about some computer story, or some website coming out. Most of my friends in college were leaving to start their own dotcoms. That was the glamorous thing to do."[13]

Stephens decided to start his own computer-repair company that would offer decent customer service.

"I was going to homes and offices and hearing the same things: 'You know I like you better than that other guy—you show up on time. You don't talk down to me. You don't smell bad,'" he said. "Now you know customer experiences are bad when that's all you have to do to surpass them. I thought, well if that's all I have to do, maybe I could do that business because there is no competition."[14]

Stephens initially named it "Techno-Medic" but decided it sounded like he repaired medical equipment. In the spring of 1994, Stephens settled on "The Geek Squad," a tongue-in-cheek nod to the image of a techie who would never be mistaken for Brad Pitt but nonetheless knew everything about his profession.

"The image of a geek is someone so dedicated to a particular field of study that, because of that focus, they allow the rest of their life to degrade—to an almost humorous effect," Stephens said. "We are so dedicated to this that we live it. After work, we all go home at night and play with our computer. How many people get off work and go home at night and play with their sledge hammer?"[15]

Aside from their uniforms, Geek Squad agents drove distinctive cars dubbed "Geekmobiles" and carried badges with titles like "Special Agent" and "Inspector." (Stephens was Chief Inspector and Special Agent No. 66.) Geek Squad's distinct, quirky culture caught the imagination of Hollywood with television shows like NBC's *Chuck*, where the title character leads the "Nerd Herd" at a big-box retailer called "Buy More."

The real Geek Squad agents had also come to embrace their professional personas.

"I had no idea what kind of effect the uniform would have on employees as they did their jobs," Stephens said. "It transforms them and allows them to play that role. I've already set up the customer with the expectation that these guys are a little odd—that's why they are good; that's why you want to use them. That allows them to be themselves, but to also play this character."[16]

But as successful as Geek Squad had become, it could have been better, Willett said. Armed with a unique brand, Best Buy enjoyed a near monopoly on mass consumer electronic service, something that Walmart or Circuit City couldn't or wouldn't match.

Yet Geek Squad oddly remained a silent presence at Best Buy. Yes, everyone recognized the uniforms and the cars, but Geek Squad agents were relegated to home visits or tech-support desks near the rear of stores. No one apparently thought to put the Geeks, Best Buy's most unique asset, front and center.

Apple Inc. would beat Best Buy to the punch. The hardware and software maker opened its first stores in 2001, which featured a "Genius Bar" where highly trained employees offered free tutorials, advice, and repair services to customers.

Sound familiar?

The idea for Genius Bar came from Ron Johnson, the former Target merchandise executive hired by Apple CEO Steve Jobs to launch the retail business. Johnson wanted to model the stores' tech support team after the kind of service a customer would receive at a fancy hotel's concierge desk.

Ironically, Jobs thought "geek" was a better way to describe Apple's techies, according to Walter Isaacon's *Steve Jobs*, a biography on the late Apple founder.

"You can't call them geniuses," Jobs told Johnson. "They're geeks. They don't have the people skills to deliver on something called the genius bar."[17]

A decade later, when it debuted its smaller "Connected Stores," Best Buy essentially acknowledged that Apple stole its thunder. At the center of each store is a long counter staffed by Geek Squad agents with the rather dry name "Geek Squad Solutions Central."

"Technology is an amazing place to be right now for Best Buy," said Josh Will, a company vice president who oversees Connected Store development. "But it's still too hard for consumers to use. It's difficult to get a good understanding of what technology can do for you and more importantly how it can better your life. It's time that our shopping environment matches that expectation."[18]

Best Buy could have said the same thing in 2002.

"We could have become the number-one service brand in the world," Willett lamented. "We would be called Geek Squad globally and we would have some stores called Best Buy. Now everybody offers services. It was a massive missed opportunity."

Today, Best Buy hopes Geek Squad can find more opportunities.

"If you look at the portfolio that we're working on today, it's really evolving into how do we help clients unleash the potential of their consumer electronics: how do we help them to empower and enrich their lives through the use of technology?" a top Geek Squad executive said. "Underpinning this, clients still need to have the security that if something does go wrong, I can go to this amazing capability called Geek Squad that has been trusted by its client base for 20 years. As part of the overall Best Buy transformation, Geek Squad is focused on how it will continue to innovate, be relevant, and provide solutions to its clients for the next 20 years. Will Geek Squad still be successful in the future if we don't innovate across the portfolio? The answer to that is, of course, no."

The executive said he wants to position Geek Squad not as a store-based tech support desk that sells extended warranties but rather as a trusted group of experts that can link the digital devices and services in the consumer's home.

"I'll give you an example," the executive said. "I had DirecTV in my house recently. DirecTV did a good job. Trouble is, they impacted my Wi-Fi network. I then had to bring someone else in to resolve this and the connected audiovisual infrastructure. In essence, the client is being asked to be the systems integrator for the consumer electronics environment within their homes, within their Connected Homes. I would pay for somebody to be my mini systems integrator, and the natural capability required to fulfill this resides within the Geek Squad today."

"When I talk about the Connected Home, it isn't just my computers and my Wi-Fi network, it is my Smart TVs, it is my wireless audio systems, it is my heating control systems, my ventilation and air conditioning systems. It may well be control of my blinds. It may well control my lighting. It may be the security system. It's this idea of providing a mini systems integrator solution across the Connected environment that is my home. We haven't tapped that potential as yet."

The Geek Squad executive also said that Best Buy might look at partnerships with insurance companies as a way to tap the home and auto market, where tech firms like Apple and Microsoft are competing to link cars to the Internet so drivers can seamlessly make calls, find directions, and listen to music.

AFTER HIS TIME AT YALE, Brad Anderson concluded that Best Buy didn't need a new strategy as much as it needed a new way to develop strategy. From this thought came the concept of "Customer Centricity," in which employees at the store level would determine what products Best Buy sold and marketed, not executives sitting in their offices.

At first, the stores that implemented the idea had shown increased sales as Blue Shirts sold more products per transaction than their regular counterparts.

But critics later said Customer Centricity was an expensive, enormously complicated theory that focused on big-box stores when Best Buy should have built out its e-commerce capabilities to take on Amazon.com.

"It was misguided," concluded Spieckerman. "And if it's misguided and you get everyone behind it, it's a fatal distraction."

Customer Centricity significantly redefined the role Blue Shirts played at the stores. Instead of selling products, Blue Shirts now had to act as mini executives, using their knowledge of the store's customers to develop strategies that would appeal to those shoppers. If those strategies worked, Best Buy could adopt those ideas throughout the entire company. Essentially, each store would act as an innovation laboratory.

"The intent was initially that most of the innovation will come out of the stuff that the stores can do pretty much on their own with variables that they control within the context of the store itself," Anderson said. "If they've got a chance to substantiate their hypothesis, they can move that test into other stores, and if they get enough momentum underneath that they can make it as a general recommendation for the enterprise."[19]

For example, employees at a store in Pasadena, California, in 2005 noted that suburban moms frequently shopped at the location, according to a case study by Harvard University Business School professor Ranjay Gulati.[20] So they decided to reconfigure the store, moving small appliances down onto lower racks along the store's main walkway, rather than leaving them stocked on higher shelves among the major appliances. The employees created product displays that showcased items such as refrigerators, stoves, and washers and dryers in homelike settings along the perimeter of the appliance department. They also created a child play area.

That's a lot responsibility for entry-level employees, many of them teenagers and young adults, making around $10 an hour. It also required massive amounts of re-training.

"A lot of our employees are high-school students, or people usually without advanced education," Anderson said. "So we started teaching employees the basic financial foundation to the business."[21]

From the input of the Blue Shirts, Best Buy broke down its "best" customers into five major segments:

- "Jill"—a suburban soccer mom who wants to enrich her children's lives with technology and entertainment. She wants to buy educational software and digital cameras to shoot and store images.

- "Barry"—a wealthy professional who likes big home theater systems.
- "Buzz"—a young techie who demands the latest electronics and entertainment like DVDs and CDs.
- "Ray"—a family man (teacher, firefighter, policeman) who wants practical technology solutions to his daily life.
- Small business owner—this segment would buy routers, switches, and computer equipment.

By identifying each segment lifestyle, Best Buy hoped to generate more sales per transaction. It wasn't just about sales of individual products but rather how those products related to each other in the context of those lifestyles. For example, Barry is probably likely to entertain his friends for Monday Night Football. So in addition to a widescreen television and surround-sound speakers, Barry would want to buy a microwave to heat up the Cheez Whiz and a PlayStation console to play the latest Madden video game.

"Selling a solution versus selling a single item is like the difference between a layup and a three-pointer in basketball," said one salesperson in the Harvard case study. "It's all about maximizing the score."[22]

But such mass customization (an oxymoron in itself) would seem to negate the very advantages of big-box retail: cost control through speed and efficiency. Each of Best Buy's 1,100 stores at the time operated by itself to target any combination of the five customer segments that shopped at those locations.

Logistically, it was a nightmare, Doyle said. Ironically, the stores lost the freedom to innovate, the core tenet of Customer Centricity, so they could focus on those five customer segments.

"It was very controversial," Doyle said. "Instead of customer centricity, it became customer segmentation. This customer really shops more in this store so we're going to change what we do here because we're more likely to have this customer come to this store. It was very complicated and even more complicated when you're in a supply chain because you're dealing with a lot of goods."

"Honestly, when this first started, I am not kidding you, it was bad," he continued. "Just for these particular stores that were participating in the tests, someone would just say, 'I need this washing machine and I need it in the store tomorrow because that so-and-so person that's going to shop in the store is going to want to see that.' Just seemed like we had a lot of people making a lot of decisions causing a lot of people to run around and move product and I don't know that the leadership was all that good during that particular project."

Customer Centricity also made it hard for Best Buy to advertise. How could Best Buy effectively use mass media—television, newspapers, radio—if each store essentially operated on its own?

The five customer segments were "customers nobody could differentiate," George Lapouch said. "Advertising wasn't customized. An awful lot of money, millions, went into a blind alley."

Under Dick Schulze, the retailer grew into a multibillion dollar company but continued to behave as an unsure upstart. The company did not develop new executive talent beyond the core group of Blue Shirts that worked with Schulze from the beginnings of Best Buy. The insular culture crippled the company just as Internet powerhouses like Apple and Amazon began to steal sales away from the big boxes. Brian Dunn, who cut his teeth as a store salesman, happened to be the wrong CEO at the wrong time in retail.

CHAPTER 4

"I HOPE I WAKE UP SMARTER"

IN DECEMBER 2011, A BEST BUY EXECUTIVE HANDED SCHULZE A disturbing letter from an employee.

Several employees suspected CEO Brian Dunn, who is currently married, was sleeping with a 29-year-old secretary who worked at the Best Buy leadership institute and sat a few feet from Schulze's own office at corporate headquarters in Richfield.

Dunn and the woman often spent time together alone in his office and outside work, grabbing drinks on weeknights and weekends. Dunn scored free tickets to concerts and games for the woman, a big sports fan whose Facebook profile pic at one time showed her posing with Ricky Rubio, the star Spanish point guard for the Minnesota Timberwolves.

The relationship made other employees uneasy, even resentful. The letter put Schulze in a bind. Normally, company policy dictated Schulze should immediately notify the board about such behavior. But Schulze decided to confront Dunn himself.

Like Schulze, Dunn never attended college. But he was a hard-working Blue Shirt who quickly ascended the corporate hierarchy, eventually replacing Brad Anderson as CEO in 2009. In many ways, Schulze thought of Dunn not only as a loyal soldier but also as a mirror image; they were both gifted salesmen who lacked a gift for strategy but showed real balls and grit in the trenches.

"Dick saw some of himself in Brian," said Wade Fenn, a former top Best Buy executive. "No college. A homegrown leader."[1]

The allegations surrounding Dunn couldn't have come at a worse time for the retailer. Though chief rival Circuit City had filed for bankruptcy, Best Buy was under attack by Amazon and Apple, not to mention a weak economy. Many inside and outside the company started to doubt Dunn's leadership, including to a certain extent Schulze, who had personally championed Dunn for the job. A scandal now would only hurt the company.

Prior to the Great Recession that began in 2008, Best Buy seemed to be performing well. Customer Centricity appeared to be working: the company's revenues had more than doubled from $19.6 billion in fiscal 2002 to $45 billion in fiscal 2008. Circuit City, Best Buy's chief rival, had filed for bankruptcy, solidifying Best Buy as the top consumer electronics retailer in the country.

"Customer Centricity is the key reason why Best Buy has survived in the tumultuous consumer-electronics marketplace, while Circuit City is gone," Ranjay Gulita, a business professor at Harvard University, wrote at the time.[2]

But beneath the surface, tension mounted in the boardroom. With Anderson set to retire, the directors debated who should replace him. Throughout Best Buy's entire history, only two men—Schulze and Anderson—occupied the CEO office; both were store veterans who spent their entire careers at Best Buy. It seemed highly unlikely that Best Buy would deviate from that formula.

The smart money was on Brian Dunn, the former Blue Shirt, district manager, and now chief operating officer. He was a gifted salesman, a loyal cheerleader, and a relentless bulldog all wrapped into one employee. Schulze loved him.

Dunn, a bear of a man with thin mustache, sure knew how to fire up a crowd. In the 1990s, the company would fly in its best salesmen for an all-expenses-paid "Achievers Party" at the Hard Rock Cafe or the Portofino Bay in Orlando. For three to five days, Best Buy would provide the Blue Shirts free tickets to Universal Studios and even rent out Islands of Adventure.

"They'd tell you why you were here, how great you are, that you're the face of Best Buy," a former top advertising executive said. "Then Brian Dunn would come out and it was as if he was a rock star to all these people. People would be out of their seats. He absolutely had this charisma. He'd be pacing the stage, talking and revving them up. He had this cadence. He held the center stage."

However, Dunn was a doer, not a thinker. He always felt more comfortable executing strategies than crafting them.

"Details and strategy weren't really his thing," Matt Henderson, the former Blue Shirt, said. "They wanted him to sell warranties. And he went out and beat the hell out of the numbers. There wasn't any thinking or discussion on should we do this or what's the best way to do it. 'You want this? Okay, I'll get you this.'"

"Brad Anderson and Tim Sheehan [another Blue Shirt who became a top executive] were very much thinkers," Henderson continued. "People really liked Tim and Brad in the stores. They were good listeners and good communicators and they seemed to see the big picture. They had the buddy-buddy network going and Dunn was a part of that clique. These guys were out of the Minnetonka store. They were always a little bit more special."

But retail had dramatically changed since Dunn started as a store clerk 30 years ago. Best Buy didn't need a cheerleading salesman; it needed a CEO with the smarts and vision to successfully guide the company through one of the most tumultuous periods in American retail, an era where technology and vision, not salesmanship, determined winners and losers.

"Dunn was an extremely hard worker but who was never equipped to transform the company," former VP of strategy George Lapouch said. "He was steeped in the culture of retail with no perspective of how to transform the company to the informational-digital age."[3]

Even more alarming, Dunn, a married man with a reputation for chasing women, lacked self-control.

"He was a hound dog," Henderson said. "Everyone knew that. You could tell that he was living hard when he was outside the store."

Still, Schulze and Anderson backed Dunn for CEO. With a little coaching and support, they figured, Dunn could succeed. And so in 2009, just as the global economy started to crumble, Dunn became CEO of the world's largest consumer electronics retailer.

From the beginning, Dunn wrestled with doubt. The night before his first day, he paced the grounds of Best Buy's sprawling corporate headquarters in Richfield.

"I hope I wake up smarter," he thought.[4]

As the global financial crisis gained steam, Best Buy's revenue began to flatline as companies laid off workers and consumers slashed spending.

Dunn seemed unsure of what to do. He was erratic, telling investors that Best Buy would close its big boxes in China only to later reverse himself. He sent conflicting signals on whether Best Buy planned to drastically cut prices during the holiday shopping season.

At times, Dunn appeared out of touch with the economic crisis. During earnings conference calls with analysts, Dunn insisted Best Buy commanded "explosive" growth potential even as the company's same-store sales deteriorated.

On Wall Street, whispers about Dunn's job security grew. CNBC commentator Herb Greenberg named Dunn one of the five worst CEOs of 2011. Forbes also called for Dunn's dismissal.

But Dunn still enjoyed Schulze's support. And as long as the founder/chairman was in charge, Dunn wasn't going anywhere.

But once allegations of an affair surfaced, Dunn officially resigned and Schulze stepped down as chairman. The board appointed director G. "Mike" Mikan as interim CEO.

"Dunn's indiscretions, they speak for themselves," Lapouch said. "Can they be used as an excuse to get rid of him because he couldn't do the real job? Yes. There was a big sigh of relief when there was a convenient way to get rid of him."

Meanwhile, Mikan took his interim role seriously, crafting a long-term strategy to rescue Best Buy.

Mikan, whose grandfather played for the Minneapolis Lakers before the team moved to Los Angeles, was young and ambitious. He had little retail experience, having spent most of his career at UnitedHealth Group, where he served as chief financial officer and later ran its Optum unit. Mikan joined the Best Buy board in 2008.

During the company's annual shareholders meeting, Mikan said his top priority was to eliminate "showrooming," the idea that people would examine merchandise in the store only to buy it online later at cheaper prices. He also urged Best Buy to reduce square footage, expand Geek Squad into additional markets, and grow further in China.

Schulze proposed the company go private and recruited Brad Anderson and Al Lenzmeier to advise him. The leadership team could best fix Best Buy outside the harsh glare of Wall Street, he said.

"Since founding the Sound of Music in 1966 and opening the first Best Buy branded store in 1983, I have believed in Best Buy and its future," Schulze wrote the board. "It goes without saying that I care deeply about the company's customers, employees and shareholders—and I will always do so....Bold and extensive changes are needed for Best Buy to return to market leadership and has led me to the conclusion that the company's best chance for renewed success will be to implement these changes under a different ownership structure."

"I cannot emphasize strongly enough how much I would welcome the opportunity to do what is best for shareholders and Best Buy," Schulze continued. "I believe there is an urgent need for Best

Buy to reinvigorate growth by reconnecting with today's customers and building pathways to the next generation of consumers. I feel that the transaction I am proposing would be a 'win-win,' as it would allow shareholders to receive compelling value for their shares, and it would allow Best Buy to take the actions that it needs to take outside of the public sphere."[5]

WHEN IT COMES TO RETAIL THESE DAYS, there are two general schools of thought. One group believes that although retailers always face disruptive change, the keys to success remain the same: excellent customer service, convenience, assortment, and value.

But others argue that something has inherently changed this past decade. The convergence of high-speed Internet, social media, and game-changing innovations led by Apple has quickened the rate of disruption to breakneck speeds.

"I think in many industries in history, you just kind of knew the path," said Jeff Jones, executive vice president and chief marketing officer at Target. "We're going to go here. It's going to look like this and we're going to do it in this cadence and these are the things that will allow us to achieve that and that's a strategic plan. People just did that."

"In today's world, the cycles of innovations of things that are impacting humans, let alone impacting retail, are just faster than ever," Jones said. "Given the pace, transformation, and change, you've got to help people understand a place we're headed, but also create the environment and the comfort level with the ambiguity of what that actually means."

For big-box retailers, adapting to that speed of disruption is a tough task, especially when your stores are generating tens of billions of dollars of sales every year.

"I was a big advocate for the Internet but not everyone in the company was at that time," said former Target vice chairman Gerald Storch, who led efforts to create Target.com in 2001. "It was a big transition back then. You had many big department stores that didn't even have to sell on their website at all. People were wondering where this is going and how would you make money but I fought hard to make it happen. I had a lot of critics but there were also many people supporting it. Especially they tend to break down on the age lines where the younger people knew it was the way of the future."

To Anderson's credit, he correctly realized that Best Buy faced existential threats when he first sat down at Yale in 2002. Best Buy, he figured, needed to tap the mind of its Blue Shirts—many of whom were in their twenties and teens—to capture the pulse of the consumers.

"That 19-year-old kid can see things that I can't—even if they're right in front of my nose," he said.[6]

But Anderson's strategic response—Customer Centricity—still proved too slow for the vast technological challenges already eroding the company's market dominance.

For all of Customer Centricity's supposed ability to predict customer behavior, the strategy failed to anticipate how quickly shoppers would migrate to online rivals like Amazon. Ironically, Customer Centricity's success depended on the Blue Shirts' ability to glean insights from store shoppers. But the Internet ultimately stole those very shoppers.

With Customer Centricity, "it was 'empower the Blue Shirts,'" Fenn said. "But the Blue Shirts aren't going to compete against an aggressive force like Apple. When it came to value migration, on how to integrate all of this, Best Buy completely missed it. It stuck with its old business model."[7]

Customer Centricity also couldn't forecast how Apple innovations in digital music and mobile devices would drive Best Buy's core products—televisions, desktop computers, and DVD/CD players—to the brink of irrelevance.

To be fair, very few people could have predicted the phenomenal success that Amazon and Apple have enjoyed over the past 15 years. In its infancy, Amazon was a curious experiment in e-commerce that focused on books. Apple enjoyed a loyal customer base but controlled miniscule market share in hardware and software compared to the likes of Dell, IBM, and Microsoft. Both companies were led by strong-willed visionary leaders who literally transformed industries and created new ones. But those kinds of leaders are more the exception than the rule.

Jeff Bezos was originally a physics major at Princeton University before switching to computer science. At age 26, Bezos joined D. E. Shaw, an investment firm founded by electronic trading whiz David Shaw, who charged Bezos with finding new business ventures.

One thing particularly caught Bezos's eye. In the early 1990s, early Internet browsers like Mosaic and Netscape Navigator allowed users to easily traverse the Word Wide Web, a communication system that connected web pages through hyperlinks. With a potential growth rate of 2,300 percent a year, the Internet offered some lucrative possibilities.

From this idea emerged Amazon, a way for shoppers to quickly purchase everything from books and music to clothing and toys with the help of innovations like user reviews, algorithms that suggested items to buy based on past purchases, and the ability to complete a transaction with the click of a button. Even more remarkable was the technology Amazon deployed behind the scenes: high-tech distribution centers that rely on computers and robots to quickly find, package, and ship to customers an endless array of products.

Nadia Shouraboura was developing algorithms and software for energy-trading firm Exelon when she received a call from Seattle-based Amazon. Born in the former Soviet Union, Shouraboura was a math whiz who received a PhD from Princeton University before joining Diamond Technology Partners and J. P. Morgan's wireless division. Based on the East Coast, Shouraboura said she'd never heard of Amazon when she flew out to Seattle to meet Bezos in 2004.

"There were so many great people," Shouraboura said. "I was just blown away and the company was moving very fast and they were doing really cool things. I just fell in love with them. Jeff's definitely a high-energy and very happy person all the time but to me that wasn't what was important. What's important was that he was very sharp, very smart."

By the time Shouraboura left Amazon in 2012 to launch her own retail startup Hointer, she oversaw the technology that powered Amazon's warehouses, fulfillment centers, and supply chain.

"What was exciting is how much we grew in terms of the number of categories we handled, in terms of the geography we cover, in terms of the supply chain capabilities and getting items to you the same day if you're in Tokyo or second day if you're a prime member here in the United States," she said.

At Amazon, the company embraced technology on both the front and back end of their business, a stark contrast to traditional retailers where techies often played a secondary role to merchants and marketers.

"If you think about the daily decisions made by the company, most of them are made through technology," Shouraboura said. "Technology decides where we're going to open warehouses, how much product we are going to buy, how we're going to fulfill it, which warehouse is going to fulfill it. It's fascinating because in many companies, it's humans who are making the decisions and at Amazon, it's driven by the computer brain."

At the same time, all that technology existed for one purpose: the customer.

"I wouldn't say that Amazon is successful because of technology," she said. "I think Amazon is very successful because it's obsessed with customers, so every decision you make is driven by thinking about the customer and it just happens that technology is a very, very powerful thing to meet customer expectation with a very high probability and to provide a very good experience. It's a computer delivering products to customers, and great cost and great selection, great convenience. Amazon was just very consistent at executing and thinking about solving customer problems."

Amazon's expansion into clothes, electronics, and toys, categories previously dominated by Walmart, Target, and Best Buy, have placed enormous pressure on those mass retailers. A study by consulting firm Kantar Retail estimates that 40 percent of Target shoppers from June to August 2013 also shopped at Amazon.[8]

Amazon has also pioneered innovative services like its Prime loyalty program, which offers users unlimited free two-day shipping in exchange for a modest annual fee.[9]

"I think Amazon has built a great product and a great experience, and so I think they are raising the bar for all retailers, pure play and physical," said Target CMO Jones. "I think there's cross shop because they're creating a nice product."

This is hardly a sudden phenomenon: Amazon has been chipping away at big-box dominance for quite some time. From January to August 2013, 66 percent of Target customers tracked by Kantar also shopped at Amazon, a significant jump from 33 percent during the same period six years ago.[9]

"Amazon's encroachment on Target has really skyrocketed," said Amy Koo, a Kantar analyst. "Target has had to compete against Walmart for many years. The challenge for Target today is to meet what Amazon is delivering to customers."

That won't be easy. Despite Amazon's reputation for low prices, consumers don't really perceive it as a low-end discounter, she said. Instead shoppers assign a premium image to Amazon, similar to that of Target.

Amazon, not Walmart, is now the single biggest threat facing Target, Koo concludes.

Apple has also left its mark on big boxes with a string of innovative devices like the iPod, iPhone, and iPad that reshaped the consumer electronics business.

By 2001, Steve Jobs wanted to move Apple beyond personal computers. He envisioned the PC as a "digital hub" where consumers could use the computer to manage photos, videos, and music they acquired or generated through mobile devices.

At the heart of Apple's strategy was to control and integrate every aspect of its products: from hardware and software to marketing and distribution.

Music seemed especially fertile ground. At the time, there was no good way for consumers to buy, share, and listen to digital music. As a result, illegal downloads courtesy of site-to-site sharing sites like Napster and Kazaam wreaked havoc on the recording industry.

So with the consent of major record labels, Jobs created iTunes' online music store where consumers could purchase music for a simple price of 99 cents per song. While Apple essentially broke even on the iTunes service, the company generated enormous sales from its iPod, which was specifically designed to work with iTunes.

"In order to make the iPod really easy to use, we needed to limit what the device itself would do," Jobs told Walter Isaacson in the biography. "Instead we put that functionality in iTunes on the computer. For example, we made it so you couldn't make playlists with the device.... So by owning the iTunes software and the iPod device, that allowed us to make the computer and the device work together, and it allowed us to put the complexity in the right place."[10]

The first iPod, called the Shuffle, was the size of a stick of chewing gum and could hold 1,000 songs. "One thousand songs in your pocket," Apple's marketing slogan went.

While iTunes is now the largest music retailer in the world, it was seen as a huge risk back in 2001. For one thing, would consumers, who could easily download music from the Internet for free, accept a legal service that charged for the music?

Even Jobs seemed to have some doubts: just building something doesn't necessarily guarantee its success. iTunes was so fundamentally new, Apple needed a way to instantly legitimize the service to millions of customers across the country at the same time. So Jobs approached Best Buy, its biggest supplier, with an intriguing offer: Apple would give the iTunes store to Best Buy for free (though Apple would still control its content) and the two sides would split the revenue evenly. In return, Best Buy would agree to exclusively use iTunes as its digital music platform.

"He rang us up and said, 'I need distribution. I have got this thing called iTunes and I only want some cut of it,'" a former top Best Buy executive said. "'I don't want all of it, I'll give it to you, you can have iTunes.' We could use it in the stores. He would give us 50 percent of the revenue of each song and we did not have to pay for anything."

Best Buy declined the offer.

"Our corporate development people under the then-chairman, said no and that was that," the former top executive said. "They didn't understand it. Some of the things that we said no to, you will be shocked. It's a cultural issue in that we don't know what we don't know and we are not prepared to, we don't like listening to other people."

In fact, Best Buy tended to see suppliers, even powerful ones like Apple, as opportunities to lower costs rather than as true strategic partners. That's why Apple decided to launch its own retail stores, said former chief information officer Robert Willett.

"No doubt about it," Willett said. "They couldn't get what they wanted from us. You can't blame them. Apple has always been open to some people. They opened more to us because we had a bigger relationship with them. But in the end, our relationship with them would be adversarial."

Today, e-commerce is so ingrained in our culture that it would be easy to say that big-box retailers like Best Buy and Target should have invested more resources into the Internet back at the turn of the century. But big boxes still make tons of cash. Even today, despite its problems, Best Buy generates $852 of revenue per square foot compared to $444 for Walmart, $305 for Home Depot, and $303 for Target, according to company documents.

For all of its growth, Amazon's business is not terribly profitable. The company almost ran out of cash in the late 1990s as it expanded into other categories and opened more distribution centers across the country. Then the September 11, 2001, terror attacks and the dot-com collapse the following year made Internet stocks all but untouchable. With once-hot startups like Pets.com and Webvan biting the dust, brick-and-mortar chains like Best Buy, Target, and Walmart looked mighty appealing.

And it wasn't as if Best Buy and Target ignored the Internet. Both companies launched websites in 2001. But building an online business from scratch is extremely difficult, especially back in the early days of e-commerce when retailers were not yet sure what products consumers would purchase on the Internet. Books were a good idea because they can be easily packed and shipped. But clothes and perishable items like food seemed less obvious because shoppers typically like to personally examine such products.

Target, along with several other retailers, decided to outsource their websites to Amazon.

"In 2001, running a website wasn't necessarily a retailer's expertise," said former Target.com president Dale Nitschke, now managing partner with the Ovative/Group consulting firm in Minneapolis. "We chose to allocate our team members toward figuring out the business, merchandising, doing online marketing, doing the things Target was better at than running a tech platform. We rented space in [Amazon's] warehouses rather than build our own because we didn't know how big it was going to be."[11]

Best Buy, however, decided to build its website on its own. Disaster ensued as the project lost more than $100 million during the first years of its operations.

"It was so trial and error," Shawn Doyle said. "We made our big attempt and it just failed the first time. It was like having this big party and nobody came. After the first Internet bust—my in-laws have a cabin in Wisconsin—and we met this guy there from New York, a big investor for Charles Schwab. He asked me, 'What do you think it's going to take to make the Internet work?' and I said, 'Logistics.' The company that's going to succeed is the company that can get the product to the customer because right now, nobody can get the product to the consumer."

Except for Amazon.

"Everybody tried to get in fast but they didn't figure out the back end of it," Doyle said. "'Okay, great, we got all these sales, now what?' How do we get them to the customer if UPS won't take something big? What if somebody orders a 60-inch big-screen TV? What are we going to do? Not only that, but if you got on the website, you could be waiting for an hour for your order to process. I could just imagine our IT guys. It had to be like *Star Trek*: 'Scotty, we need more power!' 'I'm sorry Captain! I'm giving you all she's got but I don't think she can take any more!' "

Despite its rocky start, e-commerce has certainly grown up in recent years. In 2012, total Internet sales have jumped 51 percent to $186.2 billion from $123 billion five years prior, according to comScore.[12] Combined, Walmart, Target, and Best Buy generate less than $10 billion in online sales, company figures show.

Big box is not only behind in digital commerce but the profound growth of the Internet has siphoned traffic and sales from its physical stores. Compounding the problem: slow innovation and mature product categories like televisions and computers make a trip to a store less compelling.

In 2012, U.S. factory sales of televisions and displays totaled $16.6 billion, a 36 percent decline from four years prior. And despite the launch of Microsoft's next-generation Windows 8 operating system in 2012, worldwide shipments of computers made by the likes of Lenovo, Hewlett-Packard, and Dell fell 3.5 percent to 352.7 million units from 365.3 million units the previous year.[13]

At the same time, online sales of movies and music has soared at the expense of CDs and DVDs. iTunes was so revolutionary because it allowed consumers to pick and choose individual songs instead of requiring them to purchase an entire physical album of several songs.

Digital music downloads grew 8.6 percent to $2.9 billion in 2012 from $2.6 billion in 2011, according to the Recording Industry Association of America. During that same period, physical music dropped 16.5 percent to $2.8 billion.[14] Americans now consume more music from the Internet than CDs and records.

In other words, fewer consumers have visited big-box stores because they are less impressed with the products that they see. As a result, shoppers that want to pull the trigger will do so from the comfort of their online connection at home where they can easily compare prices and, thanks to innovations like iTunes and iPods, instantly enjoy their music.

Product innovations, though, are cyclical. Things might be slow for a few years but then someone develops a breakthrough product that instantly ignites sales again. Led by former CIO Robert Willett, Best Buy instantly seized upon the smartphone craze by developing a specific format in 2010 to sell both the product and related services like activation, Internet connections, and apps. Best Buy Mobile, which operates inside each of the company's 1,000 big boxes as well as in over 300 stand-alone stores, now generates about 30 percent of Best Buy's domestic operating profit.

But retailers have now copied Best Buy Mobile. And though tablets and smartphones represent a nice growing business for Best Buy, more than 80 percent of the company's $50 billion in annual revenue still depends on mature categories like televisions and PCs.

BROADER ECONOMIC FORCES ALSO CONSPIRED to undermine big-box supremacy, starting with a basic reality: the format had run out of physical space to expand.

Take Target: in 2007, the company opened 103 new stores in the United States. Five years later, that number fell to just 25 stores. There are only so many places in America you can profitably build a 100,000-square-foot store. It's no wonder that Target is frantically searching for new revenue by expanding into Canada and growing its online business.

At the same time, fewer people are shopping at existing stores, which means lower sales per store.

From 2008 to 2012, Target's average sales per square foot rose just 1.1 percent on a compound annual growth rate. Walmart fared even worse: a 0.6 percent decline, according to company figures.

Best Buy's struggles have been even more dramatic: from $953 per square foot in 2006 to around $852 today. Building and operating large boxes requires a lot of capital, especially for Best Buy, which, unlike Target, leases its locations. Somebody has to pay the rent each month for all of that space.

So why are people not visiting big boxes? Part of the reason is the growing popularity of online rivals like Amazon. But a recent major economic event may have fundamentally altered consumer psychology: the Great Recession of 2008.

Although the United States has technically recovered from the recession, growth remains painfully slow and unemployment stubbornly high, a dual phenomenon that appears to be reality for years to come. As a result, even consumers who have weathered the recession relatively well have been visiting big-box stores less frequently and buying less.

For example, about three out of every ten shoppers told Kantar researchers they visited a Target fewer times than they did the prior year. The top reason was the same regardless of income: consumers were just shopping less in general.[15]

Interestingly enough, post-recession sales have remained more or less consistent even as traffic has dramatically dropped off, according to ShopperTrak data.[16] This suggests people are buying more products per trip at the stores that they do visit. But what type of stores are they visiting?

Research suggests that since the Great Recession, Target and Walmart have been losing customers to online stores and club/warehouse retailers like Costco. But the dollar-store format in particular has emerged as a major threat to big-box chains.

In Walmart's case, that shouldn't be too surprising since the discounter and dollar stores tend to attract consumers focused mostly on price.

But Target faces a more complicated situation. Over the years, Target has become synonymous with "cheap chic" retail through its exclusive limited edition partnerships with top designers like Missoni and Nate Berkus in clothes and home furnishings. The idea is to offer luxury-like goods at prices affordable to the broader public. Thanks to its department store heritage and formidable marketing skills, Target has carefully staked out a unique position as an upper-scale mass discounter. Hence its well-known tagline: Expect More. Pay Less.

But since the Great Recession, Target's cheap chic strategy has failed to provide much noticeable lift to same-store sales. For example, Target's holiday collaboration with luxury retailer Neiman Marcus in 2012 missed the mark with consumers, who seemed more interested in discounts than affordable luxury. In addition, other retailers have widely copied Target's trademark design partnerships, crowding an already crowded market.

In fact, Target's best performing categories of late consist of everyday household items like groceries and health and beauty products. That puts Target into direct competition with the likes of Walmart and Dollar Tree. Target's hybrid high-end-discount business model has suddenly become more complicated as the retailer battles competitors across multiple formats and channels.

With consumers today more firmly focused on so-called "non-discretionary" items, Target has had to adjust the meaning behind Expect More. Pay Less.

"Expect More and Pay Less was written a couple decades ago and the reason why it was written is that we had to find a way to differentiate from the competition on something more than price," Jones said. "It was a way to frame that when you come to Target, those two things come together. That's the sweet spot for who we are and when we're at our best."

"Today, the way we understand it, people's expectations to pay less is rising and the challenge for Target is how do we still deliver both of those things in one shopping experience," he continued. "If we are selling the leading national brand in a commodity's category, we have to make sure you're getting the best price possible. Expect More means consumers expect there are more ways to save at Target. Expect More doesn't always have to be fashion and frivolity. Saving a lot of money, getting a great deal should be an expectation as well."

RIGHT BEFORE LABOR DAY 2013, the Best Buy board made a shocking announcement: interim CEO Mike Mikan, the presumed frontrunner, did not get the job. Instead, the board hired Hubert Joly, the CEO of travel hospitality giant Carlson. Mikan eventually left Best Buy to work for Eddie Lampert, who owns Sears and Kmart.

Joly was a surprise choice for several reasons. Wall Street knew little about the Frenchman. He never worked in the retail industry. Joly, however, forged a reputation throughout his career as a turnaround specialist who favored quick and decisive action over empty bravado.

"We need to readjust our say/do ratio," Joly said during his first week on the job. "That is, we need to say less and do more."[17]

He was very familiar with Best Buy: as head of Vivendi's video game unit, Joly often spoke with the retailer's top brass, including Anderson. As CEO of Carlson, Joly even recruited Anderson to serve on the board.

Joly was also a skilled diplomat. During his first months at Best Buy, Joly took care to praise Schulze to journalists and investors. Joly kept Schulze's buyout team in the loop as he built his senior leadership team. He portrayed himself as a humble servant, whose top responsibility was to serve shareholders, including Schulze.

"As CEO, you have to work with employees, vendors, and shareholders every day and Dick is our largest shareholder," Joly said. The buyout effort "didn't change anything. I would have had to build a relationship with Dick, buyout or no buyout. Dick is our founder. He is our largest shareholder. No matter what happened, he would still be our founder and our largest shareholder."[18]

Schulze, though, was not easily swayed. Joly seemed to represent the type of person Schulze naturally distrusted: a former consultant with fancy college degrees and no retail experience. He wasn't even an American citizen. What did Joly know about the retail business?

Joly's friendship with Anderson proved crucial to breaking the ice. Schulze initially rebuffed Joly's overtures but Anderson urged the founder to engage the new CEO.

"I had not had the pleasure of knowing Hubert," Schulze said. "Brad spoke very highly of him."[19]

Schulze agreed to meet Joly on the day before Thanksgiving for their first extensive talk about the company's future. To Schulze's shock, Joly entered his office and immediately handed Schulze his resume. It was a remarkable show of respect and humility that scored Joly major points with the founder.

"In a sense, he was applying for the job," Schulze said. "That meant a lot to me."[20]

As the men began to chat, it became apparent that the two were in sync. Rather than blowing up the business as critics urged, Joly believed Best Buy's problems could easily be fixed with the right mix of leadership and discipline. Most importantly, Joly would not close stores. The big box, Joly said, was not only the historic business of Best Buy but also the company's most crucial asset to compete in the digital age.

"I became more confident that Hubert looked at the business much as I do," Schulze said. "Yes, there is a place in the world for a real-life experience where consumers can touch, feel and understand what we sell."[21]

Schulze was sold. He dropped his buyout bid and rejoined the company as chairman emeritus.

Best Buy was once again whole.

Part II

THE PRESENT AND FUTURE

CHAPTER 5

WALK BEFORE YOU CAN RUN

IN NOVEMBER 2012, BEST BUY CEO HUBERT JOLY HAD SCHEDULED a presentation for financial analysts in New York, the first time he would meet investors face to face. But Hurricane Sandy, the biggest hurricane to strike the northeast in over a century, had other plans, forcing the company to push the event back a week.

Best Buy faced its own perfect storm of sorts. The company faced an alarming decline in traffic and sales, just as Dick Schulze seemed poised to launch a hostile takeover bid. Its stock price fell to the high teens from $60 a share just two years earlier. Best Buy, critics argued, had to drastically remake itself or be in danger of bankruptcy.

Joly strolled to the stage at Best Buy Theater in Times Square and offered his plan: there would be no blowup of its business model. There would be no radical restructuring.

The problem with Best Buy, Joly argued, was Best Buy. The potential was still there. The company just needed to learn how to operate as a retailer again. Joly felt that by correcting some basic things, Best Buy could significantly improve its prospects.

"While we need to eventually reinvent the business, there is some really good, low-hanging fruit," Joly told the crowd. "The good news is that most of our problems are self-inflicted and we can and will fix them."

Such a just-do-it-better speech doesn't exactly fire up skeptical investors. The stock barely budged that day.

Almost a year later, Joly once again strolled onto a stage, this time to speak to a group of district and general store managers in Nashville.

"If all of these shirts were red," he joked, gazing at the sea of Blue Shirts that filled the audience, "we would be in Communist China. Or Target."[1]

Joly had good reason to joke. Since that investors' meeting in New York almost a year earlier, Best Buy stock had more than tripled to just below $40 a share. Sales were stabilizing, as evidenced by a flat performance during the holiday shopping season the previous year.

Normally, flat sales wouldn't be cause for much celebration. In Best Buy's case, flat meant the company was no longer *losing* sales, which in some ways was just as good as gaining sales.

"There was a rumor that we were dancing on the tables because of the flat comps," Joly said. "I'm here to tell you that rumor was true."[2]

"What Wall Street really appreciates is we're not just saying what we are going to do but we are actually doing it," he said. "Our stock price will go up and down but over the long term, great things will happen."[3]

Up until now, Best Buy hadn't exactly killed it from a sales perspective. But stock prices usually reflect a company's growth potential and investors are seeing a lot of upside in Best Buy.

Take its website, for example.

Like most brick-and-mortar retailers, Best Buy hadn't invested much time in its e-commerce business over the previous decade. But bestbuy.com was especially bad, since the company had decided to build the site itself in 2001 rather than outsource it to Amazon like Target did.

The search engine and interface did not show the same commitment to customers as the brick-and-mortar stores, as evidenced by the eight steps it took to complete a purchase. There were no product reviews and bestbuy.com frequently listed products as "out of stock" even though a nearby store carried the item. For a company that prided itself on selling the latest technology, Best Buy seemed way behind the curve.

"Our site was embarrassing," Joly said.[4]

Amazingly though, Best Buy is still the tenth-largest retail website in the country and attracts over a billion visits each year. But the website faced a glaring problem: relatively few people actually bought anything.

In fiscal 2012, bestbuy.com generated about $1.3 billion in sales. Based on its annual traffic, that means only 1.3 percent of visitors made a purchase, a shockingly low conversion rate for such a major retailer. By comparison, Staples and Amazon boast a 10 percent and 4 percent conversion rate respectively.

The formidable task of rewiring bestbuy.com fell to Scott Durchslag, who joined Best Buy in October 2012 as e-commerce chief. Durchslag had previously served as chief operating officer of Skype and held top leadership positions at Motorola's mobile unit, but his work as president of Expedia is what caught Best Buy's eye.

Under his tenure, Expedia launched its next-generation website and mobile platforms, which significantly converted more online visits into sales of hotel and air packages. Aided by its acquisition of mobile travel startup Mobiata, Expedia's software for iPhone, iPad, and Android devices became top free travel apps on iTunes in 46 countries. From a technical standpoint, Expedia under Durchslag was able to boost its ability to test its website by over ten times its previous rate, which means the company could roll out its new digital products at a quicker rate and with fewer bugs. Durchslag also plugged Expedia's "website leakage," in which online sites inadvertently leak customer data to outside hackers. That effort helped Expedia save about $20 million.

Durchslag's experience with designing consumer-facing web and mobile sites that convert visitors into paying customers, as well as the backend operations that power those systems and protects customer data, made his skills ideally suited to Best Buy.

At first, Durchslag was perplexed at bestbuy.com's low conversion rate. But as he dug deeper, Durchslag discovered that customers were using it as a research tool rather than a place to purchase products. While far from ideal, at least Best Buy had something to work from.

"The kind of traffic a website attracts is conditioned in no small part by what consumers expect to get from you," a top e-commerce executive at Best Buy said. "This is a consequence of our incredible brand awareness and consideration, that when people shop consumer electronics, they come check our site and they check Amazon. Some would check two or three other sites as well but we were always in the top consideration set."

"They may have just been coming to check price," he continued. "Then they would think they could get a lower price from Amazon. You got a lot of people just conditioned to come do a quick price check or just come get information and then actually go buy it somewhere else."

Best Buy estimates about 90 million customers want to buy something on the website but don't for the following reasons (in order of importance):

1. Need more product info
2. Product was unavailable
3. Price was too high
4. Need to see in person
5. Not available for store pickup
6. Shipping will take too long

The executive knew that none of these problems were beyond fixing. The company estimated that just boosting its conversion rate by one point could generate an additional $250 million in operating income. Or look at it another way: imagine if those 90 million uncommitted visitors spent $250 per trip, the average basket size at bestbuy.com, several times a year.

Best Buy needed to improve the basic functions of the website before designing a new platform, a top e-commerce executive said.

"We're really starting with blocking and tackling things that are not sexy, are not cutting edge," the executive said. "Frankly, it's about catching up to where the site should have been. Because if you really go through the site, in some ways, it's a ten-year time warp."

The company focused on testing its systems so that it can quickly fix problems and add new features. In the past, it would take Best Buy about two to three weeks to make changes to the website. Now it takes the company about 20 to 30 minutes

"This is about building an open, adaptive web platform that lets us rapidly test, iterate, and learn," the e-commerce executive said. "If you're Amazon, you're doing hundreds of tests a month. Best Buy only had the capability to do a handful of tests a month. What we are able to do on this new platform is to be much faster in terms of the pace of innovation."

The most glaring problem was the search engine.

About 70 percent of Best Buy's customers interact with the retailer first through the website, compared to 30 percent for stores. In fact, the e-commerce executive calls bestbuy.com its "real front door."

But a substandard search engine means customers are not finding the information they need to make a purchase. The e-commerce executive discovered that if he searched for an $800 Nikon D5200 digital camera, the engine would spit out information about a $90 Nikon Coolpix. According to the American Customer Satisfaction Index in 2012, Best Buy's website rated 77 out of 100 for browser satisfaction and 79 out of 100 for purchase intent.[5] Those scores put bestbuy.com near the bottom of the pack among specialty retailers.

Best Buy upgraded its search engine, adding 25 additional variables into a customer's search, including brands, price, and product recommendations.

"Our search engine has a new main feature—it finds products that you are looking for," Joly said.[6]

In addition, Best Buy is currently working on "contextual browsing," which allows the retailer to target specific promotions and deals to customers based on their geographic location, preferences, and shopping histories.

"You want to give them things like personalized recommendations that make it easy for them to get the stuff that they're really interested in," the e-commerce executive said.

Best Buy also more than tripled its number of customer reviews and added up to ten online "buying guides" in November 2013 for key holiday categories like televisions and computers.

To speed up the checkout process, bestbuy.com now allows customers to buy something within three clicks; still not the one-click process offered by Amazon but much better than the eight from years past. Again, like Amazon, Best Buy's checkout also features recommended products based on purchases of other customers.

For example, the website will recommend to a shopper that purchased a $300 television that he also buy an HDMI cable based on the knowledge that another customer bought the same accessory when he purchased a $8,000 3D HDTV. Despite the large price gap, the cable works with both televisions.

"We need to be able to give them a great discovery and information experience," the e-commerce executive said. "Look, to be honest, we get a lot of traffic. A bigger chunk than I probably like actually is just people purely coming for informational reasons. But you know what, they're coming directly to us."

"If we are serious about being the preferred authority and destination for consumer electronics, we need to give them the information that they're looking for," he said. "Then whether they come into the store, or convert on the site, make it as easy as possible for them to take the benefit of that information and for us to be able to translate that into a sale. It doesn't matter where it happens."

One major barrier to sales has been price, or at least how consumers perceive prices. Best Buy estimates that 29 percent of shoppers think its prices are more expensive than other retailers, compared to 13 percent for Target, 8 percent for Amazon, and just 3 percent for Walmart.

To eliminate that perception, Joly decreed that Best Buy would match any competitor's price. While such a policy inevitably erodes profit margins, the company really had no choice, Joly said.

"I don't want to lose a sale because of price," he said.[7]

To fund such "price investments," the company hopes to cut hundreds of millions of dollars over the next several years through improving its inventory systems and workplace efficiencies.

For example, Best Buy reworked its supply chain so that its distribution centers fill orders for both its stores *and* its website. Such a move also allows Best Buy to add more products to its online product list. Christopher Horvers, an analyst with J. P. Morgan, estimates Best Buy would have doubled the number of online stock keeping units (SKUs), or each individual product, to 100,000 from 50,000 in 2011. By comparison, each Best Buy store carries about 6,000 to 7,000 SKUs.

If all of this sounds like pretty standard stuff, well, that's the point. Best Buy can't offer Web 3.0 if it can't even do Web 1.0 or Web 2.0.

Joly admits Best Buy has been slow to capture the online opportunity. In fiscal 2012, Best Buy controlled 18 percent of total sales among physical retailers but just 7 percent of online sales, according to company figures. In other words, there's no shame in playing catch-up, especially when it can generate significant results.

Granted, the top e-commerce executive concedes, brick-and-mortar retailers couldn't have foreseen the exponential growth of the Internet back in 2001. That would have required billions of dollars of investment into something that may or may not have panned out over the long run. But the real crime, according to the executive, is that traditional retailers failed to respond to the online phenomenon once it had crystalized around 2006. By focusing on predicting *what* the customer wanted to buy through Customer Centricity, the retailer missed the real shift in consumer thought, which is *how* they want to buy things.

"It is beyond arrogant I think, within Best Buy, to say, 'We have the power to change whether the consumer buys online or in the store,'" the e-commerce executive said. "If the consumers are going to go online, they're one click away from anywhere. They're going to shop where they want to shop. The whole future of retail is being able to shop when, where, and how you want. Particularly with Millennials and some of the younger demographics that are going to be really important to us. That's the way they think."

Best Buy, however, isn't just copying other online retailers. The company has two distinct advantages over competitors like Amazon that it plans to integrate with bestbuy.com: loyalty and customer service.

Best Buy boasts one of the largest customer loyalty programs in the country with over 40 million members, about four times larger than Amazon Prime. But Reward Zone, as it was originally called, operated on a separate online platform from bestbuy.com. Amazingly, the two sites did not share the same customer database and did little cross marketing.

"Drove me crazy," the e-commerce executive said. "It was mindblowing."

Tying the loyalty program, now renamed My Best Buy, to the website allowed the company to better collect customer data so it can design specific offers and experiences for its best shoppers.

"We can't personalize offers to you if we don't know who you are," the e-commerce executive said. "All that's tied into our knowing your history so that we can surface stuff that's relevant to you, and it all requires us to have known who you are. That is going to move sales conversion dramatically. By bringing My Best Buy and bestbuy.com together, we have seen the number of people logging into the website explode. It was remarkably simple to do."

Best Buy also redesigned the loyalty program. It doesn't cost anything to join My Best Buy and basic members can receive free shipping for every purchase of $25 or more. Amazon Prime members pay an annual fee in exchange for unlimited free shipping.

"It cost $85 to join Amazon Prime," Joly said. "$85 is not free shipping."[8]

More importantly, My Best Buy doesn't simply reward customers with discounts and offers for just buying stuff. The program also wants to incentivize shoppers into specific actions both on-line and within stores, like writing product reviews, visiting the Samsung Experience store-within-a-store concept, or redeeming gift cards.

"We really reconfigured the loyalty program to make it a vir-tual currency," the e-commerce executive said. "Because that's your sort of passport across all of the different touch points of the Best Buy experience. You want that unique identifier, because you're going to be getting points and have the ability to get expe-riences too."

Another untapped pool of potential revenue is Geek Squad. Like Reward Zone, Geek Squad existed in its own online bubble, with no connection to bestbuy.com. If Blue Shirts at a Best Buy store tried to sell customers accessories, installations, and warran-ties to complement that purchase of a PC or television, wouldn't it also make sense to do the same thing online?

Best Buy is working to integrate Geek Squad into its web-site so that the company can recommend and sell packages or "bundles" of products and services that can enhance the value of a single purchase. Again, it seems like an obvious strategy that somehow eluded Best Buy, despite the fact that the physical stores have been doing this for years.

"Geek Squad is our secret weapon because Amazon doesn't have Geek Squad, Target doesn't have Geek Squad, Walmart doesn't have Geek Squad," the e-commerce executive said. "It's like having a personal shopper, to go back to the depart-ment store analogy. There's an expertise there that'll become only more valuable to consumers as things get more complex in working across competing platforms like Apple, Microsoft, and Google."

Best Buy is exploring ways to integrate live Geek Squad agents into the website. For now, shoppers can communicate with Best Buy's regular customer service reps on live chat boxes. But the e-commerce executive says the website can perhaps offer the chance for consumers to ask Geek Squad agents for help through video conferences via Skype. Geek Squad could be the deciding factor that pushes a visitor over the finish line into a paying customer.

"Where I think we want to go, is to be thoughtful about these consumer electronics discovery tools and experiences," the executive said. "This is stuff that I don't believe Amazon would be willing to invest in because they sell products across many different categories. Whereas we are focused on consumer electronics and the tools to help you pick a camera, which is very different than the tools to pick a mobile phone. We could bring a video chat experience into the process at the right point in the funnel to help trigger a sale."

When you add it all up, Best Buy has left a lot of online money on the table that's now ripe for the picking with some intuitive adjustments to the website.

Like Best Buy, Target has been playing catch-up with its website. Today the website generates about $2 billion in sales, but still lags far behind Walmart and Best Buy. By comparison, Amazon generated $31.7 billion in website sales.

Target has also struggled with turning its 300-million-plus unique visitors a year into paying customers. The retailer's 1.9 percent sales conversion rate is only slightly better than Best Buy's.

Even worse, Target's own customers prefer to shop at Amazon than the Target website: 64 percent of Target's monthly in-store shoppers went to Amazon versus 20 percent to target.com, according to Kantar Retail.[9]

But while Best Buy's website has been relatively quiet over the years, Target's website has been thrust in the spotlight, and not for good reasons. In 2011, Target, realizing the growing power of e-commerce, decided to retake control over its website after outsourcing operations to Amazon for a decade.

The company hired Sapient Nitro, a digital marketing agency, to revamp its website to include enhanced product reviews, social media, and quicker checkout. The new target.com debuted that summer but soon met disaster.

For a year, Target had been planning a collaboration with venerable Italian fashion house Missoni, best known for its colorful zig-zag patterns. It was Target's most ambitious design partnership yet: a collection of 50 items of clothes and accessories and, thanks to Target's vaunted marketing machine, celebrities and regular shoppers alike clamored for the limited supply of merchandise.

But when Target launched the collection in September, the website proved no match for the frenzied demand the company itself created. Target.com quickly crashed and was down for several hours. Over the course of that day and several days after, customers complained of slow online access, delayed shipments, and long wait times to contact customer service. In some cases, target.com had accepted credit card payments for orders only to cancel them later because the products were no longer in stock.

It was an embarrassing setback for Target; instead of basking in the glow of its most popular design partnership yet, the company struggled with an onslaught of bad publicity.

It would have been perfectly understandable for Target to hit the "pause" button while it licked its wounds. Instead, the company pushed full steam ahead with its digital makeover even while it worked the bugs out of target.com.

Following the Missoni debacle, the retailer made significant investments in money and talent to strengthen the speed and stability of target.com and improve the search, navigation, and checkout process.

"Are we playing catch-up?" said Casey Carl, Target's digital chief. "Yeah, with where our aspirations are, absolutely. That's where the gap stands. We've got some things to work on. The website experience isn't where we'd like it to be. It's certainly not on par with our store experience yet. But we've made huge strides in terms of sales conversion. With that said, we still have some opportunities to really show off some of our more basic content on the website: better product descriptions and reviews, the right color swatching, and showing more how-to videos."

And just as Best Buy is integrating Geek Squad and Reward Zone into bestbuy.com, Target is also working on ways to better use its formidable marketing machine to push e-commerce sales.

Whether through product guides, videos, or Bulls' Eye View, Target's online newsletter, the retailer likes to give its shoppers a behind-the-scenes look at the people who create Target's trademark design collections and advertising campaigns.

"Our content, especially around apparel and style, is absolutely critical to our long-term vision, where we can truly differentiate ourselves," Carl said. "Our marketing point of view is just some of the areas where we exposed content that is uniquely Target."

"Whether it's our collaborations with Philip Lim or Jason Wu, consumers want to see, 'How did Jason Wu design all those garments? What was the back story there? How did you arrive at this design collection?'" he continued. "They are already consuming those pieces of content. We absolutely think there is a brand element to it, but I believe it's already driving sales, and we'll continue to really accelerate that."

Target has also long enjoyed strong relationships with Hollywood and the music industry. The company is a major partner with the Grammy Awards and the American Film Institute. Over the past several years, the retailer has sold albums with exclusive bonus material, including extra tracks from Justin Timberlake, Taylor Swift, and Beyonce.

But given the growing popularity of digital content, Target executives say they had to move beyond physical media like CDs and DVDs. In fall 2013, the company launched Target Ticket, where shoppers can download movies as well as music with those extra songs from the website.

"The exclusive content formula really works, but we have a bunch of our guests that say, 'I want that formula, but I want it the way I want it, which is digitally,'" Carl said. "The ability to really consume content on any of your devices and interact with target. com, that's where we want to go with it. Then it's the question of how big do we want to make it. Because if you drew an ecosystem around the physical and the digital, our market share in entertainment is huge. It's really important to our guests, especially guests with families. We know that physical will slowly go away in our guests' mind, but that's going to take a long time. We've got to deliver both options because we have guests that only want physical."

Eventually, Target wants to use its expertise in creating and distributing entertainment to offer a premium service like YouTube in which consumers pay a higher price for even more material like additional songs, music videos, and behind-the-scenes footage.

The company is also doing something it has not done in 15 years: make acquisitions. Since 2013, Target has purchased Cooking.com, CHEFS Catalog, and DermStore.com, a beauty website. Not only will Target integrate those websites' content, products, and services into target.com and gift registry, the company also plans to create new ways for consumers to interact with brands and each other. One idea under consideration is a portal where consumers can upload and share recipes.

"Where we want to go long term is thinking about those websites as experiences and brands that our guests can access wherever they want," Carl said. "Tomorrow you'll see more branding pages, you'll see more shared things. That's what Cooking.com is really good at, so why would we go out and try to do that ourselves? Why not just leverage something we already own and share that with all of our guests?"

Target and Best Buy face significant challenges in digital retailing. Before the companies can focus on next-generation technologies, they first needed to master the basic things, like creating a decent search engine, incorporating product reviews online, and just making sure the websites don't crash. Such low-hanging fruit offers the chance for the retailers to convert more online visitors into paying customers.

CHAPTER 6

ROOM TO ROAM

ON AUGUST 16, 2012, HUBERT JOLY FIRED OFF AN EIGHT-PAGE MEMO TO the board of directors at Best Buy.

The company should not be in a hurry to close stores, wrote Joly, at the time a top candidate for CEO.

"Of course I would need to look at the profitability of the individual stores but we also would need to take into consideration the fact that the company was going through hell for a number of months, not years," Joly recalled writing. "I thought the company could be reenergized and therefore the profitability of the stores was going to be what we would make of it. In a business like this, if the strategy is to shrink," it would mark the beginning of the end.

Three days later, Joly got the job.

Joly's stance seemed pretty counterintuitive at the time. Just two months prior, his predecessor pressed to close more stores. Wall Street and critics looked at Best Buy's 1,000 big boxes not as assets but rather 1,000 ways to drown in costs. As more consumers shifted to the Internet, Best Buy would be left holding the bag of expensive store leases it could no longer pay for.

"Now sometimes you have to cut some limbs for the base end to survive," Joly said, "but I was really hopeful that I would not have to do this. It would damage morale if you have to tell employees and vendors that you're going to reduce the floor space by 30 percent over the next five years as opposed to saying we're going to save all of these stores because we're going to make them profitable."

The question was how to convert all of that cost-draining space into gold.

One thing that surprised Joly was the symbiotic relationship between Best Buy and its manufacturers like Microsoft, Sony, and Toshiba. Each desperately needed each other to survive, though that mutual need tended to get lost in the daily haggle over price and credit terms. For many companies, Best Buy accounts for anywhere between 30 percent and 70 percent of their overall sales.

Throughout its history, Best Buy succeeded in putting much of its competition out of business. If Best Buy, which controls 15 percent of the consumer electronics market, were to go belly up, how would those companies distribute their products? Sure, they could sell over the Internet or open their own stores like Apple. But selling things is an entirely different (and perhaps more difficult) business from making things. From picking the right locations to designing an optimal store, it could take manufacturers several years to build a national chain of brick-and-mortar locations that would justify the cost.

During his first week on the job, Joly said that Best Buy must work with its suppliers to give customers prone to Internet shopping a compelling reason to visit its stores.

"It's like a game," Joly said. "We have this space. How do we maximize the contribution from that space in a way that's good for the customer and economically feasible? It's an interesting puzzle to solve, but not one that can't be solved."[1]

He cited how luxury vendor Ralph Lauren worked with Macy's to create attractive Lauren displays throughout the department store.

"That's something I want to explore," Joly said. "As a major retailer, we are very important to our suppliers. There's got to be things that we can do for their benefit and for our benefit. There are partnership opportunities, exclusive products or other things. I look forward to meeting with these guys."[2]

Meanwhile in Seoul, South Korea, J. K. Shin, co-CEO of Samsung Electronics and also its head of mobile business, took note of Joly's remarks. Thanks to its well-received Android-based Galaxy line of tablets and smartphones, Samsung had emerged as a formidable competitor to Apple and its iPhones and iPads.

The company had considered launching its own stores in the United States but decided against it. Building the stores could take three to five years and Samsung needed to capitalize on its momentum.

Shin had an idea: why not open mini Samsung stores within the Best Buy box? Such a store-within-a-store concept, which is popular in Asia, could help Samsung immediately sell more products in America without the time and expense of building its own stores.

In early December, Shin flew from Russia to the Twin Cities and pitched his idea to Joly over dinner in the strategy room of Best Buy headquarters in Richfield.

"I'll focus on the products and the innovation," Joly recalled Shin telling him, "and you do the retail. We will not open stores. We will concentrate only on products."

"And we will not launch our own phone," Joly replied.

To Joly, the emerging deal was a windfall. For one thing, the concept, called the Samsung Experience, would be exclusive to Best Buy, adding a jolt of excitement to a chain that really needed some. Best Buy would hitch its wagon to one of the hottest technology brands in the world.

"It was very clear that they needed us and that we thought that from a customer standpoint it would be great," Joly said. "They thought the economics were great for them and of course we thought the economics were great for us."

Samsung would essentially rent space from Best Buy and provide staffing and marketing support. Best Buy would benefit from customers drawn to the Samsung Experience, who would then presumably shop the rest of the store.

"The store-within-a-store idea is a creative strategy," said Keith Anderson, a consultant with RetailNet Group in Boston. "If you're having a tough time getting paid by consumers, who else may have money for you? In this case, it's big brands that don't like the way their brands are presented on the web. They also know that people want to see the product and talk to somebody before buying. They know it's a much higher risk and commitment to go launch their own flagship stores."

"Now all the mobile guys like Verizon have their own stores," he continued. "Increasingly you see other device makers opening their own stores. But Best Buy still gets an amazing amount of traffic. This alternative shared risk/shared reward model versus the traditional 'I'll buy inventory from a manufacturer and mark it up and make a margin on each transaction' can be a long-term viable idea, if it can offset the declines in traffic and sales conversion at retailers like Best Buy."

In one swift move, Best Buy, which was struggling to make productive use of its enormous space, found a strategic partner willing to pay the retailer for something Best Buy already had.

"The thing made so much sense," Joly said. "In retail, you normally want to test an idea first. But sometimes you come from a pretty bleak situation, you're a little bit bolder. In fact, the name of the project was Project Bold."

By the end of the dinner, Joly and Shin shook hands on a deal. Eight months later, nearly all of Best Buy's stores in America boasted a Samsung Experience shop.

"The companies decided to move forward extremely quickly because that's part of the Korean culture," Joly said. "It's really impressive how fast they are moving."

Store-within-a-store concepts are not new. They have long been a staple at high-end department stores in the United States and Great Britain. Bloomingdale's, for instance, features stores-within-a-store from Ralph Lauren, Calvin Klein, DKNY, and Kenneth Cole. Selfridges & Co. in London arguably pioneered the model. Such stores are common in China but the retailers act more like landlords who mostly keep the lights on.

Over the past few years, more retailers in the United States have started to explore deeper partnerships with outside vendors. Ron Johnson, the former CEO at JCPenney, championed the store-within-a-store idea at the department store chain before the board ousted him for poor sales.

Target has struck a more cautious tone, preferring to keep control over its store experience. But the retailer has recently used outside parties to provide customer service in electronics, baby, and beauty departments. Target even launched Shops at Target, special sections throughout the store that featured merchandise from boutique shops around the country.

Best Buy has arguably been the most aggressive proponent of store-within-a-store even before Joly joined the company. Magnolia and Pacific Kitchen, two high-end retailers Best Buy had acquired in previous years, form the heart of Best Buy's next generation "Connected Stores."

In this smaller format box, Magnolia, which sells home theater equipment, and Pacific Kitchen, which offers pricey appliances like Viking ranges, each occupy distinct stores staffed with their own employees. Combined with Best Buy Mobile and Geek Squad stations, a Best Buy today looks more like a shopping center than a single consumer electronics chain.

Such concepts can pay off under the right circumstances. A recent study by Carnegie Mellon and the Wharton School of Business at the University of Pennsylvania suggests that the store-within-a-store carries truly differentiated merchandise. "If it drives more people into the store, it's attractive," the study said. "Retailers will go for it more often."[3]

The Samsung deal stands out on its own. For one thing, all 1,000 Best Buy stores carry the Samsung Experience shop. By comparison, 750 stores carry an Apple mini-shop even though

Apple is Best Buy's largest supplier. Each Samsung Experience store, which averages about 465 square feet, carries a broad range of smartphones and tablets all sold by Samsung employees who can sell and activate the product.

Done the right way, the store-within-a-store strategy can be very successful, said Gerald Storch, the former Target vice chairman who later became CEO of Toys "R" Us.

"As long as you pick the right brands and you're flexible it's a great model," Storch said. "The key is making sure that the brand you're partnering with is trending in a positive way and important to the customer. You don't want a wrong partner. Because today's hot brand could be tomorrow's dog. You need the ability to switch it if a brand gets out of favor. If you strike the deals that are too long, then you have to keep the shop up even when the brands are not desirable anymore."

Best Buy, however, "is doing a great job with Samsung," Storch said.

In addition to quickly building out the shop, Samsung has also collaborated with Best Buy on innovative ways to promote its products. For example, Samsung struck a deal with the hip-hop mogul Jay-Z, in which shoppers who buy Galaxy smartphones at Best Buy can access his new album for free by downloading an app that "unlocks" the songs embedded in the device.

"Best Buy's agreements with Samsung take vendor relationships in an important new direction," Gary Balter, an analyst with Credit Suisse, wrote in a research report. "While Apple may have already have space dedicated to it in the store, there is little or no training support from Apple. It is not a true store-within-a store in our view."

"The new agreements may cause Apple and others to reexamine their approach, which we believe offers a source of more upside down the road," Balter wrote. "These efforts should provide improved service levels, secure access to the latest and greatest products, keep more people purchasing at Best Buy, and to point to significantly higher gross margins over time."

Since the Samsung deal, Best Buy struck similar arrangements with Microsoft and Sony. In May 2014, the Japanese electronics giant said it will open "Sony Experience at Best Buy" shops at 350 Best Buy locations across the country to showcase Sony's home theater technology.

"We welcome consumers to experience the best of Sony with a premium and unique shopping experience at Best Buy," Mike Fasulo, president and COO of Sony Electronics, said. "The Sony Experience at Best Buy will be an ideal place to inspire, engage, and educate consumers about Sony's home theater products."[4]

If there was ever a product that consumers prefer to see in person, it's a giant ultra-high-definition television. The Sony shops boast enhanced fixtures, interactive demonstration areas, and dedicated Sony employees. Using touchscreens, shoppers can control content on the TV wall and compare different models.

"The Sony Experience will give consumers a shopping experience unlike anything before," Mike Mohan, Best Buy's chief merchandising officer, said in a statement. "Sony's 4K Ultra HD televisions have to be seen to be believed. Our newly transformed home theater areas will, for the first time, allow customers to test, try, and experience how all of the Sony products work together."[5]

Google also enjoys new enhanced product displays at 500 Best Buy stores. The same goes for Beats, the premium headphone and speaker manufacturer founded by Dr. Dre and legendary producer Jimmy Iovine, at three stores in New York.

The Google partnership has sparked rumors that it will eventually open stores-within-a-store similar to Samsung and Microsoft. Joly doesn't discourage such talk. Though primarily a search engine, Google has delved deeper into physical products including Nexus smartphones and tablets, Chrome notebooks, and wearable Internet-connected devices like Google Glass.

"The new displays are a significant step forward for Google in our stores," Joly said. "Historically, Google had a small end cap where they would sell the Chrome notebook and they had their own employees showing the Chrome book. What they have now is [a] big product display in wood decorated in Google's bright colors. It's pretty close to what we have done for the Surface Microsoft tablet in terms of scale."

"It's actually quite meaningful and it's the kind of stuff that makes sense this year for them given what they have in terms of product lineup," Joly continued. "It shows how significant Google has become as a player in the tech space. You could say the Samsung store is also a Google store because its products use Google's Android operating system. As Google's physical product line expands I'm sure the dialogue will continue."

"Any brand that you think makes sense, we're probably in discussions with them," Joly said. "The stakes are high. A lot of people got intrigued when we did the Samsung announcement. Everybody said, 'Ah ha, this changes the game completely.' "

A BIG BOX'S MOST VALUABLE REAL estate may not even be its show floor. In the back of each store lie cavernous rooms where employees unload and store thousands of products that will later find their way onto a shelf or end cap.

But who says only the associated store can sell that merchandise?

Faced with the exponential growth of e-commerce, large retailers like Toys "R" Us, Nordstrom, Macy's, and now Best Buy in recent years have been using the inventory from stores to fill online orders. As with the store-within-a-store concept, the ultimate goal is to suck every drop of productivity out of space retailers already own or lease.

Instead of the usual model of shipping goods out of a handful of distribution centers, retailers can quickly reroute products from hundreds of stores located closer to homes and businesses.

In Best Buy's case, about 70 percent of its customers live within 15 minutes of a store. That gives consumers the flexibility to either pick up orders in the store or have the store ship the product to them.

"For whatever reason, more than a third of our online revenue comes from products actually picked up in our store," said a top logistics executive at Best Buy. "As we make that process more efficient in our stores, I believe that that number could potentially even grow."

"Why would customers want to pick it up in the store?" the executive said. "One: 'I travel. I don't know when I want to pick it up, but I want to make sure it's there when I want it, and I don't want to be hostage to a time frame.' They might live in metro markets, but if you don't have a concierge in your building, you won't be in a position to be able to receive the package, thus you're going to end up picking it up at UPS or FedEx instead of picking it up in a very convenient retail location. Some people don't want other people in their home to know that they purchased the product, because it may be a gift."

"Ship-from-store," which can deliver goods to customers the same day they ordered them on the website, can transform the industry, executives and analysts say.

"Each of our stores is a warehouse," Joly said. "The back of the store at a Best Buy store is actually quite large. Why? They were designed years ago when TVs and PCs were large and so there's a lot of room there. How many warehouses does Amazon have in the country? 86? And they're spending and spending to get more. We already have more than 1,000. We're making our entire inventory available from anywhere in the country and so that changes the game significantly."

Ship-from-store represents how American retailers have come full circle with inventory management. If you recall in Part I, Best Buy at its infancy was little more than a bunch of stores that raided warehouses for merchandise when managers decided they needed it.

"For a while, that was sort of enough," said consultant Keith Anderson. "It was that simple. Retailers created demand through mass media like TV, radio, and especially newspapers. If you had the store, you were good to go because the industry was nowhere near as saturated as it is today. Nobody was as focused on supply chain efficiency or the benefits of scale financially. These strategies just were not central to the way that big retailers competed back then."

That changed as chains grew into multibillion dollar operations. Throughout the 1990s, Best Buy and other big-box retailers adopted the hub-and-spoke system of logistics: build a centralized network of warehouses and distribution centers that would supply stores within a particular geographic region. The system, pioneered by Walmart, was designed to create cost savings by efficiently moving large quantities of goods from manufacturer to store. Such a rigid command-and-control model, however, did not allow for much flexibility in day-to-day operations, which made it hard for retailers to respond quickly to sudden shifts in consumer demand.

As Best Buy slowly built out its website in the first half of the 2000s, the company supplied its stores and online business from separate distribution centers. Best Buy eventually realized that it was losing out on some significant sales. Often, bestbuy.com would inform a customer that the desired item was out of stock. But those very products would be sitting on a store shelf just a short walk or drive away.

"So we've got 1,000 stores sitting with inventory and we just got done telling a customer they can't have what they want," chief financial officer Sharon McCollam said.[6]

Of the 84 million people who visit bestbuy.com each month, about 2 to 4 percent are unable to buy a product because the website says the retailer ran out of inventory. But in 80 percent of those cases, a Best Buy store carries that same product.

"Those are the worst three words on the Internet: out of stock," Storch said.

Best Buy eventually established a system in which customers can order something online and later pick it up at a store. Today, about 40 percent of Best Buy's online customers receive their orders this way.

In 2009, Nordstrom decided to take this service one step forward. The luxury company ultimately spent $100 million to rewire its 100-plus stores so that it can fill online orders with store inventory.

In the ship-from-store system, a customer buys something on the website, which reroutes the order to a nearby store. An employee receives the list of items to pick, scans a barcode, and then selects the merchandise from the shelves or back room. He then packs the order and leaves it for FedEx or UPS to deliver.

"It turns out that stores aren't that big," Storch said. "The employees know the store really well and they fill the orders quite fast if you put in some productivity tools to make sure they're not walking around in circles."

"Space is an advantage," he said. "If you're a Best Buy, Target, or Walmart, you have a physical inventory of your entire market in the actual store. The issue is, what does the customer need that you're fulfilling? If the customer's need is immediate, the store is the most efficient way to do it. There's no doubt about it."

Storch knows this issue pretty well. He launched an early version of ship-from-store at Target.

"When we started target.com, you could order a men's dress shirt from Marshall Fields," which Target owned at the time, Storch recalled. "It would come off the dot matrix printer and an employee would pick it from the shelves and send it. Department stores like Macy's and Nordstrom always had great store locator systems. They were always able keep in touch with the store to find the missing product."

Macy's, which eventually acquired Marshall Fields, recently expanded the ship-from-store system to all 292 of its stores. The company invested in sophisticated software that could accurately monitor and track inventory to ensure a store really carried the product the online customer ordered. It also helped ensure the store itself did not run out of a product for its regular store customers. Today, the service generates more than $500 million in online sales, or about 10 to 20 percent of Macy's total annual online revenue.

During the first year of the service, Nordstrom not only increased same-store sales but generated its highest inventory turnover rate in five years.

Nordstrom and Macy's were simply building out a system that department stores already had in place, Storch said.

"When you go to the department store and you want that jacket in a small size but it wasn't on the shelf, they could say, 'Oh, we have it at Southdale Mall,'" he said. "The employee would say, 'You want to get it there or we'll ship it here?' They could also send it to your home. Department stores have been doing that since we were children. They're able to tie into the systems and do it quite easily. That's why a lot of the online growth at Macy's is coming from ship-from-store."

Storch would later establish a sophisticated ship-from-store system at Toys "R" Us.

"I had the same epiphany a few years ago," Storch said. "My friends would keep asking for products that were last year's product. They'd say: 'I want this kitchen set. I went to the store, it wasn't there,' and they would have a cut out picture their granddaughter had given them. I said, 'Because it's last year['s model].'"

"But we did have it, one left somewhere in Iowa," he continued. "I would arrange it so we could ship to the friend. I started to think we could do that for everyone."

When Sharon McCollam, a former top executive at Williams Sonoma, joined Best Buy in late 2012, she quickly recognized that her new employer could easily establish ship-from-store. The company already had the necessary technology in place because of buy online, pick up in store.

"When they created this capability, they created one inventory" for both the stores and website, McCollam said. "We already had invested in the systems to do ship-from-store over the last several years."[7]

When McCollam started at Best Buy, the company wanted to install "ship-from-store" at all 1,400 U.S. and Canada locations in two years. The retailer ultimately completed the project a year early.

"We accomplished this feat because of the transformational, cultural change that occurred at Best Buy under Joly," said a top logistics executive. "You cannot unlock 1,400 stores without every organization in this company coming together around the online channel. You have to get the organizational mindset around, 'We are a multichannel retailer.'"

Through ship-from-store, Best Buy managed to offer consumers another $3 billion worth of inventory without having to spend one dime of shareholder money. Best Buy executives estimate ship-from-store was a major reason why online sales during the final four months of 2013 jumped nearly 27 percent. The company thinks ship-from-store will account for one-third of Best Buy's e-commerce sales growth this year.

"Without even trying, we became the tenth largest Internet retailer in this country," the logistics executive said. "Can you imagine what we might become when we actually are focused, and we say it's one of our top priorities?"

The executive also thinks ship-from-store can solve another nagging problem at Best Buy: product returns. The company has a 10-plus percent return rate, a number greater than 80 percent of all U.S. retailers.

Across the country, manufacturers and retailers are trying to dispose of growing piles of unsold or returned goods either through recycling, charitable donations, or selling them to outside liquidators eager to get their hands on top-quality goods for rock-bottom prices. The size of this "secondary market" is about $329 billion, or about 2 percent of the U.S. economy, according to industry estimates.

But logistics experts say those companies are essentially throwing away money, especially with product returns.

"Companies that ensure timely delivery and processing of returns position themselves to save more or earn more from the returned product," according to a report by UPS and reverse logistics firm Greve & Davis. "Returned products are often untapped sources for revenue. With the secondary discount market for products continuing to grow, there are even more reasons to think about returns as revenue opportunities."[8]

Until recently, Best Buy had no direct way of disposing of returns, replacements, and damaged goods. Instead of dedicating store space to clearance items, the retailer instead sold the products to third-party liquidators.

As a result, Best Buy loses about $400 million a year from this system.

"We are not actually selling the majority of that product," McCollam said. "We are allowing others to sell it and compete against us. So I think we can all agree that the returned, replaced, damaged opportunity is enormous."[9]

The problem is especially acute when you think of the consumer electronics business and its ever-quickening product cycles. Companies like Samsung and Apple offer new models of smartphones and tablets at an even faster clip. A consumer could buy an iPhone 5 one year only for that product to be outdated in two years when Apple releases the iPhone 6.

"The system automatically says that if you're a store with a small quantity of the outdated product, you're going to take a 30 percent markdown," McCollam said. "If you have a medium quantity, you'll take a 40 percent markdown. And if you have a lot of it, you'll take maybe a 50 percent markdown. It's almost systematic at Best Buy."

"By opening up buy online, ship-from-store, obviously it doesn't matter where the inventory is sitting," McCollam said. "We have a billion visitors a year coming to our website and you can move the inventory that way."

But Best Buy boasts one strategic advantage over its competitors that can help the company sell that merchandise even faster: Geek Squad.

The company recently enlisted Geek Squad to inspect "open-box" merchandise and certify that those previously unwanted laptops and smartphones are fit to be resold. The company hopes customers that see a "Geek Squad Certified Open-Box" sticker on a returned product will feel more comfortable that they are not purchasing a broken or defective item.

"Our customers do have very high trust and faith in Geek Squad," said Geek Squad chief Christopher Askew. "Clearly, it gives customers who seek to purchase open-box that trust and confidence that the product will function as exactly as it should, as new. Open-box [products] are attractive to value-orientated customers who are looking to save money and still get access to top brand, knowing that Geek Squad has put its stamp on it."

"Specific to consumer electronics, we are exposing customers to something that is distinct and unique," he said. "We're not just putting opened-box items out on the floor. It actually goes through a robust inspection process by a Geek Squad agent on site."[10]

To boost confidence in open-box items, retailers often turn to outside firms to certify the products as sound. But that takes time and in the fast-moving consumer electronics industry, today's hot device could be yesterday's junk in a short period of time. Some secondary-market analysts say high-turnover products like cellphones can lose as much as 10 percent of their value every month.

"But what if you had Geek Squad certify it, like Mercedes-Benz Pre-Owned?" said the logistics executive. "Most retailers can't do that. They don't have Geek Squad. All of a sudden, Geek Squad is turning into another diamond in Best Buy, that we actually have not leveraged for a very long time. We can now unload the returned inventory and offer it to our customer base online."

The executive thinks pre-owned goods will especially appeal to mothers and environmentally conscious Millennials.

"There's a scenario under which it brings women to the brand, because a lot of secondary consumer electronics are actually bought for children," the executive said. "People that want to buy an iPad for their child, say a six-year-old, they don't necessarily want to buy a new iPad, because it's going to be broken."

"As for Millennials, think of eBay," she said. "eBay has probably got one of the largest secondary market businesses out there. When you look at their customer base, they are heavy in Millennials. Thus it's highly likely that Best Buy will soon be the largest secondary market seller of consumer electronics online. Thus, bringing that Millennial customer, and being able to serve a facet of the market that, today, quite frankly, we do very little in that market. It's a huge opportunity for us, going forward."

MAYA MIKHAILOV HAD A BIG PROBLEM. Actually, two big problems.

GPShopper, the company that she and her husband Alec founded in 2006, had just developed what they thought was a surefire blockbuster: software for the mobile phone that could help customers research and compare prices of products online and in stores.

But retailers balked at the idea. For one, the Mikhailovs called their app "Shoplifter," not exactly the image retailers normally want to embrace.

"We thought it was so darn clever," Mikhailov said. "What made it even worse, our motto was 'Steal this Deal.'"

The company could change the name rather quickly. The other problem—not so much. Shoplifter was simply ahead of its time.

In 2006, before there were iPhones and tablets, mobile brands like Nokia, Blackberry, and Motorola dotted the landscape. Websites were websites and phones were phones. No one had yet thought of creating apps that could bridge the two platforms.

"Alec and I originated from the mobile world but we realized it was really much easier to find things on desktop websites," Mikhailov said. "If you needed to find something you could just open a new tab to compare prices and inventory."

"But the minute you walked outside the boundaries of your house, you were really at a loss," she said. "If you wanted a product, you didn't know who actually had it and for how much, until you arrived at the store. Unless you'd decided to call all the stores in advance. That seemed so inefficient. We thought to ourselves: 'Why not take that efficiency of online shopping and combine with the real world where 95 percent of shopping still occurs, in brick-and-mortar stores?'"

So GPShopper created software that would allow users to access a store's prices and merchandise on their phone. Unfortunately, retailers did not possess reliable data on their local inventory.

"It quickly became clear that there would never be enough data," Mikhailov said. "I think at one point we had something like 2 to 3 billion products in our systems at local stores. That's still not even enough. We would need 2 to 3 trillion products."

Some retailers also feared that the app would cannibalize sales from their stores. In other words, they would shop on their phones at the expense of their websites and brick-and-mortar locations. As it turned out, the concept that GPShopper championed did cause retailers to lose sales—to outside competitors.

Thanks to the launch of powerful smartphones and tablets and the ensuing ecosystem of sophisticated apps, consumers have broadly embraced the idea of using their mobile devices to compare products and prices on the go.

"Nobody wanted to be price compared," Mikhailov said. "Retailers were like, 'Oh, this is horrible!' But now that Pandora's box is wide open, there was no going back."

Shoppers could walk into a Best Buy store, spot the price of a television, and instantly compare that price to Amazon or Walmart. Thus began the idea that customers treated Best Buy as little more than a showroom, that they would inspect the product in the store and later purchase it online for a lower price.

"The Internet has been a big deal," said consultant Keith Anderson. "But I would say mobile even more than the Internet accelerated the challenges that brick-and-mortar face. The transparency, especially around price, is the biggest or the fastest moving ship we've seen over the last few years."

But just as big-box chains used store space to exploit their vast stocks of inventory, they also found ways to adopt mobile devices as an asset rather than a liability.

"Nowadays, smart retailers are in fact embracing the empowered consumer," Mikhailov said. "They are recognizing that consumers are walking into their stores, with digital devices, and they are helping themselves to product information, whether you provide it or not. There's literally no stopping them, it's just changing fundamentally the way that consumers are interacting with brands and retailers."

Today, Walmart, Target, and Best Buy rank the highest among mobile shoppers in 2013, according to Prosper Insights and Analytics: 29 percent of consumers said they used their smartphone or tablet to shop at Walmart, followed by Target (27.7 percent) and Best Buy (22 percent).[11]

"Mobile is already a giant part of our business in terms of actual sales," a Best Buy e-commerce executive said. "It's just really exploded, perhaps more than most people would imagine for a retailer compared to other industries. But it's going to go even higher because mobile just lends itself so well to our stores and website."

As it turns out, mobile devices may be the best thing to ever happen to big boxes, a convenient "shopping assistant" to help consumers better navigate such large stores. In addition to researching products and comparing prices, smartphones can encourage people to visit stores more often and to stay longer with interactive experiences.

"We can personalize customer experiences through our in-store apps," the e-commerce executive said. "You'll start to see mobile devices as the platform by which we give you access to special promotions and events. We can instantly enable an electronic ticket on your phone to admit you into something or a coupon to receive digital content. It becomes a very powerful tool."

Deloitte Consulting recently estimated digital technologies influence 36 percent, or $1.1 trillion, of in-store retail sales, and this number will likely increase to 50 percent of in-store sales by the end of 2014. Smartphone devices alone influence $593 billion, or 19 percent of all in-store retail sales.

"Given this acceleration, we are at a tipping point in retail— a point where digital channels should no longer be considered a separate or distinct business," the Deloitte report said. "Instead, digital is fundamental to the entire business and the entire shopping experience, in and out of the store. As this new reality begins to have a greater impact, retailers should change dramatically the way they think, measure, and invest in digital and address their customers' digital needs and wants."

Here are some of the more intriguing findings from the Deloitte study:

- *84 percent* of visitors report using digital for shopping-related activities before or during their most recent trip to a store.
- Consumers who use a device during their shopping journey convert to paying customers at a *40 percent* higher rate.
- *22 percent* of consumers spend more as a result of using digital.

Even better for Best Buy, mobile devices drove the electronics/appliances category more than other kind of product, Deloitte said. Smartphones and tablets influenced 31 percent of such purchases last year, far outpacing furniture (26 percent), clothing/footwear/accessories (24 percent), and groceries (16 percent).[12]

GPShopper, which abandoned its original idea of selling apps directly to consumers, went to work designing mobile software for retailers. Today, the company manages Best Buy's "Game Stoppers" app, which allows consumers to manage their game inventory for PlayStation, Xbox, and Wii.

By scanning the video games with their phones, consumers can create online libraries, complete with product data, user ratings, and, more importantly, up-to-date information on each game's market value.

"Ultimately, with any video game, you get tired of playing with it," Mikhailov said. "You might want to trade it for another game. The app can tell you 'Hey, *Call of Duty: Ghosts* is coming out and if you trade in two old *Call of Duties* for the new *Call of Duty: Ghosts*, maybe we'll also give you maybe a special map pack.' Best Buy is essentially letting people recycle their games in a weird way. They're letting people leverage their existing collections to get early and better access to new games they might want."

Bottom line: the mobile app pushes gamers, an already fiercely loyal customer segment, to further purchase merchandise at Best Buy, either online or in store.

"This is a new type of engagement that Best Buy can have with the consumer on a very personal level," Mikhailov said. "I can just let you shop with me however you want. If mobile's your hot new thing now, then great, do it on the mobile."

"What Best Buy really proved is that mobile devices drive in-store sales and drive people to the store. Whereas the website user is maybe more of a visitor, the mobile app user is a customer. They already made the effort to download the app. Chances are, you're not going to download an app from a retailer or brand unless you're engaged with that retailer or brand. As almost any retailer will tell you, the majority of their purchases come from a very narrow audience of engaged consumers."

GPShopper also created an app for Best Buy customers to track their Reward Zone loyalty points.

"Best Buy was quite ahead of its time as well," Mikhailov said. "It was the first time a retailer had mobile enabled a loyalty program. Now you cannot get retailers to stop talking about the fact that they need their loyalty program to go mobile. You could log in to the app, check your points, check your purchase history, and see the certificates that were issued to you."

Now that Reward Zone is My Best Buy, the company has big plans on how to further integrate the loyalty program into mobile devices.

"The idea is as soon as you go into the store and check in on My Best Buy on your device, it shows you a map of the store," the e-commerce executive said. "We have flashing spots where there are products that we are recommending personally for you. We know if you're moving around, if you're not moving around. If you're staying someplace too long, we can automatically dispatch a Blue Shirt to help you."

"The employee will see on his tablet that you're an Elite Plus member," he continued. "That in the last three weeks, you were browsing the website for speakers. That you have this type of hardware in your house. He recommends products to you. If you still haven't bought anything, we make you a super time-limited exploding offer: make a purchase within the next 30 minutes at the store, you get 10 percent off."

"If I still don't have you and you're walking out the front door, I can hit you with another offer that says: 'If you go to bestbuy .com and buy that speaker, you'll get an extra 200 My Best Buy points.' We can do things like that."

For Target, mobile represents a second chance of sorts. The retailer had already missed the initial wave of desktop-based e-commerce when it relaunched its website in 2011. That target.com performed horribly during its first few months certainly did not help narrow the gap between itself and more technologically savvy retailers.

But as Target was making much-needed fixes to the website, the company was quietly building out one of the more impressive mobile operations in the industry, experts say.

Out of Walmart, Target, and Best Buy, only Target earned a positive Net Promoter Score (NPS) for its mobile efforts, according to Prosper Insights & Analytics.[13] NPS is an industry metric that measures loyalty. So while all three retailers ranked high in overall performance, only Target's customers say they would recommend the mobile site to others.

"Our mobile experience is really good," said Casey Carl, Target's digital chief. "It will be the future. Mobile is already our future. Inside the company, we've talked about how mobile is the portal to the Target universe. A Target in your pocket everywhere you go. Everything Target, accessible through the phone at any time."

The retailer enjoys a built-in advantage over the competition: most of its core customers already use mobile devices.

About 70 percent of Target shoppers own smartphones and 40 percent have tablets, according to Kantar Retail. They are more likely than the average U.S. shopper to use the full range of shopping-related tools mobile offer: nearly 40 percent of Target shoppers surveyed by Kantar said they used their smartphones over a six-month period to research a product online while in the store and to post comments on Facebook and Twitter about a potential purchase.[14]

By the end of 2014, Target expects half of all its digital traffic to come from its mobile platform.

Knowing this, Target launched in 2013 its most ambitious digital effort to date. Dubbed "Cartwheel," the company partnered with Facebook to offer digital coupons to people who frequently visit the social media site. The idea is to push Target customers into stores more often by appealing to their love of smartphones and social media.

Consumers log into Cartwheel with their Facebook accounts. They can access a wide range of discounts on everything from Diet Coke and toilet paper to flat-panel televisions and clothing. Each day, Cartwheel offers on average 800 deals with consumers taking a closer look at 780 of those discounts.

"That tells us that somewhere in those offers, there's something for everybody," Carl said. "That's the beauty of it, that it's so customizable that 20 deals that you pick are going to be entirely different than my 20 deals. Five percent off seasonal berries might be really relevant for what you need because you were just going to go buy blackberries anyway. For me, it might be something totally different."

Shoppers redeem their discounts by visiting a Target store where employees scan a special QR code on the shoppers' smartphones.

Once shoppers pick a deal, it appears on their Facebook newsfeed so other friends can see it. They can earn more discounts the more they shop or if they can successfully share their offers with other friends. As people use the site, they can earn "badges" like Super Scanner or Uber Saver to grab more discounts and perks.

"Cartwheel's the epitome of linking social activity to commerce," Carl said. "We're leveraging Facebook for what really people like to do, which is to share. Sharing your deals, or why you love Target, why is it uniquely you, why you're into these products versus other products."

So far, Cartwheel has been an enormous success. The service, which already boasts more than 2 million members, generated over $100 million in sales in 2013.

"Cartwheel's performance has been phenomenal," Carl said. "It's unlike anything Facebook has ever seen, which is awesome."

In a way, Cartwheel's success took Target officials by surprise. They knew that Cartwheel would create a lot of buzz, that it would strengthen consumers' emotional bond with the retailer. What they didn't expect was the level of commerce the service has generated. Consumers were not only visiting Target stores more frequently, they were buying more per trip.

"We thought there'd be a lot of people talking about how they love Target, our differentiated product and content," Carl said.

"They would love to share their thoughts on it. 'Hey, I just got this great dress. What do you think?'"

"What we weren't expecting is the utility usage," he said. "Half of our guests are actually using Cartwheel inside the store. Like a weather app, they're using it all of the time, to build their shopping lists and chat about their experiences."

Best Buy and Target are finding new ways to use their stores beyond simple showrooming. Both retailers are transforming their stores into mini warehouses, in which consumers can pick up online orders or the stores themselves can ship goods directly from the shelves or back rooms.

"You could argue that our stores are too big," the Best Buy logistics executive said. "Think about when Best Buy started. We had these huge, cubic televisions. Computers took up this table. Our back rooms were built in a time when the product was enormous. Now, we have all these back rooms that are completely underutilized for the current cubic size of our inventory today. What were we able to do?"

"We turned them into mini distribution centers," the executive said. "With virtually no investment at all, we were able to take those back rooms, which one might have perceived as unutilized space, and turn them into a mini-shipping operation that unlocked the entire store, and that entire store's inventory, for a customer."

Best Buy is aggressively pursuing the concept of stores-within-a-store. Through its partnerships with Sony, Samsung, and Microsoft, Best Buy wants make more productive use of its floor space while at the same time offering a unique experience to customers. In the future, Best Buy locations can position themselves as malls, where outside vendors and retailers can rent space within the big box.

But the store-within-a-store strategy indicates a much deeper shift in the relationship between big box and manufacturer.

In the 1990s and early 2000s, manufacturers were forced to sell products in chains because of the size, clout, and reach of such retailers.

One former sales executive with General Electric and Black & Decker who sold goods frequently to Target said the retailer once promoted one of his products during its two-day "Black Friday" sale in late November. The result: 95,000 units sold for $2.5 million in just 48 hours.

Vendors, however, resented how big boxes focused on squeezing profits out of suppliers. Target was dead-set on generating at least a 30 percent profit margin, the former sales executive said.

"I remember going into a room with just me and a group of Target executives, including a senior vice president," he said. "They would say, 'Your price is a little too high,' and then send you out to a waiting room with seven other vendors, whom they told the exact same thing. It was great for Target, not so much for the vendors. Nobody liked it, but that's how the game was played."

But the power of Internet retailers like Amazon have prompted big-box retailers like Best Buy and Target to treat suppliers less as profit centers and more as collaborators, not just on marketing but also on product design, Joly said.

"We want to focus on unique assortments with our key vendor partners," Joly said. "One of the things that's not known, and I think we can leverage increasingly, [is that] our teams work very closely with key hardware manufacturers on designing products."

Joly recalled the first time he and Jason Bonfig, Best Buy's head computer buyer, met Microsoft CEO Steve Ballmer.

"Jason, do you know that you decide what computers get made in the world?" Ballmer said.

"I know," Bonfig said.

"And so we are able to design unique products that have features and functionalities that we can deliver to customers and help make Best Buy a destination for customers," Joly said.

While Target still places enormous pressure on its suppliers on price, the retailer has adopted a more collaborative approach with its best vendors in recent years.

For example, Target relies a great deal on outside suppliers to develop private-label brands like Archer Farms and Market Pantry. The retailer devotes about 30 percent of its store inventory to private labels. Target's "C9" activewear partnership with Champion has been especially successful with C9 generating more than $1 billion in annual sales. Champion and Target are currently testing the C9 Active Apparel store in San Francisco, a standalone shop that features athletic apparel and gear for men and women, including yoga mats and water bottles.

But since the Great Recession, Target has also started to work more closely with national brands to develop marketing and merchandising programs that emphasize convenience and value. Internally, this strategy is known as "E4": Easy, Experience, Educational, Engaging. The retailer has been experimenting with "cross merchandising," an effort to curate products from different brands to help solve a problem or meet a need. Since 2012, Target has rolled out product displays in the pharmacy area that combine vitamins, wellness, and nutrition products. The company has also grouped together related products under sections called "Dinner's Ready," "$1 and Under," "Toy Shop," and "Giftables to Go."

"Target wants to use national brands as a reference point, to say, 'You see, we have national bands too, equally priced or comparable to Walmart; therefore, why do you need to go there?' Or, 'We're certainly better priced than Walgreens or CVS,'" said Leon Nicholas at Kantar Retail. "Ultimately for Target, they're looking for national brands to be co-partners, to be co-marketers, with their brand, the bullseye."

CHAPTER 7

"FIRE A LOT OF BULLETS"

WHEN TARGET FIRST STARTED TO DEVELOP CARTWHEEL IN EARLY 2013, the retailer had modest expectations for its social savings tool.

Partnering with Facebook, the retailer would offer daily deals to customers, who could later redeem the offers via their mobile devices at Target stores.

But something else happened. Much to their surprise, shoppers weren't just sharing deals on Facebook: they were visiting Target stores more often and buying more stuff per trip, said Casey Carl, Target's digital chief.

"That actually wasn't how we designed it," he said. "But I will tell you that we've done a major pivot from what we originally conceived it to be. About half of our guests are actually using it in-store. The best description is like your weather app. They're using it all the time as a utility app *and* as an inspirational thing where the social element really plays."

In many ways, Cartwheel represents an enormous cultural shift in Target. The product was conceived in just a matter of months by a new unit inside the company that focuses on quickly converting ideas to actual products. In addition, Target designed Cartwheel on the fly, knowing full well that the service was flawed but released it to the public anyway with the hope that it could improve the product based on customer feedback.

Normally, whether a marketing campaign is behind Taylor Swift's album or the launch of a design collection from Jason Wu, the retailer would spend years planning every meticulous detail and then launch the project with the full force of a tsunami.

But with Cartwheel, Target wanted to do something completely alien to its culture: make mistakes. The team proposed a low-key "beta launch" only for employees and some customers so the company could collect data and work out any bugs in the system before Cartwheel made its debut in earnest.

"It was a big cultural moment for Target," said chief marketing officer Jeff Jones. "We're going to put something in the world that we know is not perfect. We're going to take guest data and we're going to improve the product based on what the guest shows us they want through their actions."

"We are testing, in any given day in Cartwheel, over 100 data experiments," he continued. "We are continuously learning about how do we make the user experience better, what kind of offers do people want, how do they download the app, when do they use the app, is it pre-trip or in the store."

"In the startup world, you wouldn't get criticized for that," Jones said. "You would be told that's innovation. But Target, because we've always focused on crisp and flawless execution, we would never have done that in our past. We're demonstrating a new kind of thinking. Putting a beta product into the world is what happens in Silicon Valley every day. Of course there are things to criticize about it, but we don't take that as criticism, we take it as user feedback to improve the functionality."

IN HIS CORNER OFFICE at Target corporate headquarters, Jones keeps a copy of *The Singularity Is Near* by futurist and Google engineering director Ray Kurzweil. In the book, Kurzweil argues that technological advances like computers and the Internet will create such exponential growth that it will eventually outstrip humans' ability to comprehend the phenomenon.

"We've been very clear about our destination, of the initiatives we had to tackle," Jones said. "Keeping that same discipline and clarity is important, especially when you're dealing with several hundred thousand employees that you're trying to bring along on a journey. We just kind of knew it's going to look like this and these are the things that will allow us to achieve our goals."

"But in today's world, given the pace of transformation, you need to also create the environment and the comfort level with the ambiguity of what that actually means. The cycles of innovation that are impacting humans, let alone impacting retail, are just faster than ever. We need to create a culture of comfort with the unknown so people still are driven to go fast and are destination oriented, they want to win, they've got goals, but they also recognize that arriving there just might not be the same linear path that it used to be."

"How do you still operate with urgency, but create the organizational capability to go in a different direction fast if required to do so? That's different than just speed. That's very much a thing that all retailers are working on: how do we become more agile and not just stay fast?"

In some ways, Target, a company that prides itself on detailed long-term planning, seems ill suited for such rapid rate of change.

For example, when Target first established its website a decade prior, the move prompted much division among its management ranks. At the time, Target stores were thriving, which made it hard for executives steeped in the Dayton department store culture to understand why the company would spend millions of dollars on a project that lost millions of dollars for the first few years of its existence.

"I had a lot of arrows in my back," said one former executive involved with the website.

Jay Samit knows a thing or two about corporate infighting. As executive vice president and general manager of Sony Corp. America from 2003 to 2007, Samit witnessed the rollout of the Japanese electronics giant's stores in the United States.

The Sony stores flopped, partly because the company focused mostly on appeasing its disparate product divisions rather than thinking about what the customer would want, he said.

"Culturally, they had to figure out how do we divide up our square footage between all our different business units politically and that maybe didn't fit the model," Samit said.

Factions within large companies will fight to protect turf. And corporations find it hard to invest in new initiatives when their current businesses are still performing well, he said.

"Kodak had a division that saw the future being digital cameras, digital pictures, computers, people would share stuff digitally," Samit said. "But the big daddies making money, the big division that got you promoted into a corner office, were the people making film. That upstart's going to be losing money for a bunch of years. It's a career dead end, and if it's even the slightest bit successful, it's cannibalizing my sales and me making my bonus."

"One part of the big conglomerate tends to kill the other part that is its future," he said. "That is why there is no Kodak today. That is why IBM doesn't make machines anymore. You see this over and over again. Big corporations are not set up to innovate. Innovation comes from disruption. It comes from someone looking and saying I see a better way with technology, whatever it empowers people to do."

For target.com to survive, the company needed to remove the e-commerce team from the rest of the company so it could operate within its own culture. So Target established a separate headquarters for the website at the City Center complex, located just a few blocks north of the main corporate building on Nicollet Mall in downtown Minneapolis. The move would only breed even more resentment among brick-and-mortar managers, the former executive said.

At the time, target.com had the support of CEO Bob Ulrich. But even Ulrich grew uneasy with the project. During one meeting to review the website's numbers, Ulrich dismissed the nascent e-commerce business as "middling." To boost morale, the target. com team later wore t-shirts around its office that read "NOT a middling business."

But as Internet sales began to take off in earnest, Target recognized the need to retake control over its website from Amazon. Partnering with Sapient Nitro digital marketing agency, Target debuted the new website in August 2011, just two weeks before the retailer launched its most ambitious design partnership to date: a 50-piece collection of clothes, accessories, and home goods from the venerable fashion house Missoni.

The result was a complete disaster, as the website soon crashed and stayed dark for hours. For the customers who managed to get orders through, they soon discovered the items they bought were actually sold out even though the website had already processed their credit card information.

Others complained of long delays in receiving their shipments. In some cases, consumers received tracking numbers from Target, but UPS had no record of them. Angry shoppers berated Target on social media for the lack of prompt and effective customer service. One Facebook user created a page called "the BP Oil Spill of Fashion."

At the time, Target blamed the website woes on "unprecedented" traffic and demand. In truth, IT experts say the retailer failed to properly test its systems before it debuted the website in August.

Target gave itself little time to fine-tune its website, said Adam Roozen, a former top online executive for Sam's Club, the warehouse chain owned by Walmart.[1] Normally, businesses roll out their sites gradually, giving themselves wiggle room for hiccups and glitches. When Roozen worked at Sam's Club, he said the company rolled out its redesigned website in small increments instead of waiting to "flip the switch" all at once.

The website problems were an eerie precursor to the Obama Administration's botched rollout in late 2013 of healthcare.org, the federal health insurance exchange that underpins the Affordable Care Act. In each case, there was a major disconnect between what was promised and what was ultimately delivered, said Joshua Carlson, a data privacy attorney in Minneapolis, who formerly oversaw major IT projects at Best Buy.

Part of the problem was that while Target's vaunted merchandising and marketing teams were busy creating and hyping the Missoni collection, the website was far from ready to handle the enormous traffic from such an endeavor, Carlson said.

Part of the problem was that merchandisers and marketers, not technologists, ran the show at Target, a company that always prided itself on developing its own talent—everyone from Bob Ulrich, still considered by many as the company's best CEO of all time, to Michael Francis, the legendary chief marketing officer credited with developing Target's "cheap chic" image. The company's phenomenal success over the years has reinforced a belief that its culture is special, a place that demanded and often won an intense loyalty from customers and employees alike.

But such a culture can also be insular, to the point that a successful career largely depends not necessarily just on performance but also the power of belief. That makes it hard, of course, for employees to challenge the status quo and defy groupthinking if everyone else is drinking the proverbial Target-red Kool-Aid.

"Target is very self-referential," Leon Nicholas, a senior vice president at Kantar Retail, told a group of suppliers last year. "They like to talk about themselves. They believe their press. They are insiders in that culture who do well and are promoted. And there are folks who sort of bounce off their atmosphere and don't do as well."

But Target wasn't always so confident. When the Dayton brothers inherited the department store from their father, they realized the growing company needed professional management.

Like many of the department stores in the 1950s, Dayton's was a family-run business whose core strength was merchandising. In retail, there was no such thing as McKinsey consultants and finance executives with fancy MBAs from Harvard or University of Pennsylvania. Aside from Bruce Dayton, who once took an accounting course, none of the Dayton brothers studied business.

It was Bruce Dayton who first discovered that the American Management Association held a weeklong program for top executives at Cornell University. All five brothers took the course and were determined to apply what they learned to running the Dayton department store and later Target.

The brothers were especially focused on corporate training. In 1958, Dayton's joined with General Mills, Honeywell, and Norwest Bancorp (the predecessor to Wells Fargo) to create a school called The Four Companies Program, which taught modern management techniques to their top executives. Dayton's eventually extended training to middle managers with a three-day seminar at the Ambassador Motor Hotel.

"We were nuts on professionalism," Ken Dayton once wrote. "Perhaps because we were a family-run business...we worked doubly hard to become highly professional ourselves and to instill professional management throughout the business."[2]

It was Ken Dayton who developed the idea of "organizational surplus." Under this concept, every manager would train his or her own successor so the manager could move up and be replaced by capable talent.

"Furthermore, the achievement of organizational surplus meant the retirement of any individual would not affect the well-being of a company," Bruce Dayton wrote. "There would always be someone younger and qualified, perhaps better qualified, ready to take his or her place."[3]

Organizational surplus ensured Target would enjoy a self-sustaining pool of talent that would constantly advance and replenish its ranks. Employees are constantly measured and scored. At the same time, it's nearly impossible to get fired, employees say. If someone screws up, the company will try even harder to coach that person.

The system has its benefits: it ensures stability, consistency, and has produced a deep bench of talent immersed in the "Target Way"— past and current senior executives like Gregg Steinhafel and Kathy Tesija all started as merchants, first as business analysts before the company promoted them to buyers and inventory managers.

But outside of the C-Suite, the culture produces insularity among the rank and file and uninspired groupthink.

"Target is probably as centrally controlled a retailer as any other one out there," said Leon Nicholas of Kantar Retail. "Part of it is because of this notion that the Minneapolis headquarters makes the brand, crafts the brand, cultivates the brand, and then in effect exports the brand out to stores, and the store's responsibility is to focus on execution and compliance."

"Target is a scorecard-driven culture," he said, "the extent to which the store managers don't have a heck of a lot of autonomy to do things, to try things. Things are given to them and they must manage and operate those stores as expressions of the brand. You tend to see very consistent merchandising, very consistent execution, if not good execution, across the stores."

But over the past year, Target has been remaking its culture to include more outside voices. Starting with the senior leadership team.

STEPPING INTO THE ROLE OF CMO AT TARGET IS DAUNTING, especially if the man you're replacing is widely considered not only the best marketing chief in the retailer's history but also in retail itself.

That's the predicament Jeff Jones found himself in after Target tapped the former Gap CMO to replace Michael Francis in April 2012.

Worst yet, Jones was an outsider. People naturally assumed that Target would simply promote someone from its deep bench of marketing talent. But despite its devotion to organizational surplus, Target did the once unthinkable: hire a non-Targeter to join the senior management team and fill perhaps the most important position at the retailer outside of the chief executive.

Boyish, articulate, and energetic, Jones is a study in contrast to Steinhafel, a career company man, who shunned the spotlight and appeared uncomfortable during the one media event of the year Target hosted for reporters in New York.

"You got to have a 'go get 'em' attitude," said one former sales executive with General Electric and Black & Decker who knows Steinhafel well. "You got to be a real bullshitter. [Former vice chairman] Gerry Storch, he was an excellent merchant. He would work the room, always asking vendors what was going on, what was the next big thing. But where the hell was Steinhafel?"

Jones, though, knows how to press the flesh. He had extensive experience in both corporate and agency advertising, having worked at Coca-Cola and at the Leo Burnett ad agency. In 2004, Paul Pressler, a former Disney executive tasked with reviving Gap, tapped Jones to head its marketing efforts. Under Jones's leadership, the retailer used celebrities like *Sex and the City* star Sarah Jessica Parker to plug its clothing.

Jones found significant success at McKinney, an independent ad agency where executives praised him for his coach-like management style, digital know-how, and entrepreneurial instincts.

Jones was the brains behind "McKinney 10 percent," which required employees to spend 10 percent of their time on projects unrelated to client business. He helped Sherwin-Williams create Chip It!, an interactive digital tool that allows consumers to turn any picture online into a palette using the company's paint colors. He also launched and led Motobias, a separate unit within McKinney that helps users create dynamic video.

Target needed not just new ideas but also a new culture that could see those ideas to fruition, Jones said.

"Culture is a word that gets used a lot because it's a summation of many, many things," Jones said. "For me, culture changes when individual people change, and individual people change when they understand the context of why it's important. That's where leaders play an extraordinary role in today's world, where you can help individual people understand the need to change, and to help them through the uncertainty that comes with change."

"I've always believed that you have to start at the top and the bottom at the same time," he said. "As a leader, you've got to have leadership alignment, so you've got to have the people at the top shaping where we're headed believing the same things. That creates momentum when there's alignment. The bottom of the company, any company, is where incredible ideas are. Incredible innovations happening. People with great opinions. People that can influence others through their words and behaviors. When you create cultural movements, you have alignment at the top and you spark fires at the bottom. When you spark those fires at the bottom, things start to burn in a good way, right?"

Last year, Target opened a "Technology Innovation Center" in San Francisco, hiring dozens of data scientists, software engineers, and designers to work on next-generation products: software that allows customers to photograph products with a smartphone and get instant offers and product information, mobile devices that can automatically detect where to find a store that carries particular merchandise based on users' current locations, computers that can predict future needs based on present purchases. Unlike the first target.com, which was located just a few blocks from company headquarters, Target wanted to open a facility near Silicon Valley where they could better recruit the best computer science talent in the country.

"Retail is undergoing a major revolution," said Beth Jacob, Target's executive vice president and chief information officer at the time the innovation center opened. "Technology is key more than ever. It requires us to get comfortable with a test-and-learn mentality and innovate faster."[4]

An innovation center is all well and good but is largely useless unless the innovation moves from lab to reality.

Target is a retail giant whose hundreds of thousands of employees carry their own agendas and incentives. Merchants based in corporate headquarters, not technologists working in a remote office, tend to wield the most clout in such large retailers, Carol Spieckerman from newmarketbuilders said.

That's why "the innovation should come from the outside in, not the inside out," she said. "The San Francisco office should not just vet ideas through headquarters but challenge headquarters to rise to the occasion."

Unlike the first website, whose employees were mostly isolated from the rest of the company, Target designed a process to connect the Technology Innovation Center's work to headquarters. Every month, David Newman, a former Apple executive who runs the San Francisco office, travels to Minneapolis to brief officials on their technology "hunts." Projects are divided into three categories: core research, learnings (What's ready? What's not?), and handoffs (ideas better suited for other departments at Target). Committees of top executives vet the ideas and move the best projects forward.

At the same time, Target holds Big Idea contests for employees, in which winners receive time and money to develop prototypes for their projects. Of the 700 submissions the company received during the last contest, four projects are in some stage of production. The retailer also hosts twice-a-year TGT Make Days when techies work on whatever they want.

"We are willing to take bets on ideas that won't go forward," Jacob said. "As an organization, we are well prepared to do that."

Committees representing executives from IT, marketing, merchandise, and digital sort through the ideas. The more promising ones go to the new Rapid Application Deployment (RAD) office at headquarters, where teams develop prototypes and run small store pilots. Like target.com at its infancy, RAD enjoys its own separate office, a working space that's closely reminiscent of the innovation center in San Francisco.

One of RAD's first projects was Cartwheel.

Target also established a Stores Digital Integration team where store managers work with technologists on improving the in-store experience for customers.

Beyond specific projects and programs, Jacob said Target wants employees to naturally think about innovation on an everyday basis. So the company has made considerable investments in training, education, and work tools.

For example, Target recently launched Hi Tech, where downtown employees can attend workshops and receive personal IT help instead of relying on the telephone hotlines most companies use. The program has proved so popular that the company plans to expand Hi Tech to its north campus in Brooklyn Park and perhaps offer "roving" Hi Tech teams to other Target offices.

The company has also rolled out an internal Wiki system so employees can quickly share and access information as well as digital links to help workers connect their mobile devices to the Internet more easily.

"I'm thrilled and amazed to see the creativity of our employees' ideas," Jacob said.

Target has begun experimenting with ideas on a regular basis, even if they don't provide much in the way of sales and profits. In the summer of 2013, the company launched Bullseye University, a big digital campaign to attract college students for the back-to-school shopping season.

At the heart of Bullseye University was a makeshift dorm built on a set in Los Angeles where college-aged YouTube celebrities "lived" in rooms outfitted with Target merchandise. For three days, Target live-streamed the celebrities over a special website as they interacted with viewers over Twitter, mused over random topics, and plugged the Target gear. Website viewers could also buy certain items by scrolling their mouse over the merchandise in the dorm rooms, which activated an info box and links to purchase them.

Target wanted to test ways to fuse event marketing and social media with actual commerce. In the end, Bullseye University did not generate much in the way of revenue, but the company did glean some important insights into the coveted Millennial consumer, Jones said.

"In a world where there is no answer, we have no choice but to experiment," he said. "It's funny. If Target operated in another industry, people would call it research and development. 'Yup, you have to have a big R&D budget to innovate and stay ahead of the curve and trends.' Marketing, however, comes off as novel playing around.

"There is a lot of science we apply to optimizing every channel where we put our messages. We've got deep analytics that tell us very precisely what happens with search, with the weekly ad, with TV, all the time. Is that sexy? I don't know. Our job is to do our work as long as it works, while at the same time trying to figure out what's next.

Jones said Vine and Twitter are still relatively new technologies. "So if we're not understanding those new ways to connect, learning, and finding the potential, then by the time someone knows exactly how it works, we're probably too late."

HUBERT JOLY LIKES TO INVOKE a lot of imagery and nearly all of it relates to action or motion.

"Did I ever tell you about my bicycle theory?" he once asked a reporter. "When you stand still, you fall off the bicycle. But if you keep pedaling, you may not go the right direction, but at least you can turn."[5]

"What do they say in Chicago?" Joly said. "Vote early and vote often? I find it inspiring. We should also shop early and shop often."[6]

Pedal. Fall. Turn. Do. Say. Shop.

Those are the verbs used by a turnaround specialist who wants to create a culture at Best Buy that prizes careful but decisive decisions, accountability, and clarity of purpose. From the moment

Joly joined Best Buy, he made clear two things: he was in charge and Best Buy's singular goal was to grow same-store sales and profits in the United States again.

Nothing else mattered.

"So we said we only had two problems to solve: declining sales and declining margins," Joly said. "It could have been worse. We could have had three or four problems. We declared that our strategy and position in our strategy was to be the destination and authority for technology products and services. That's who we are."

"We set as a goal to begin to stabilize," he said. "And then after that, begin to increase our sales and our margins. In a turn-around, I find certainly that strategy follows operational progress rather than the other way around. And it's the thought that operational progress creates strategic ways of freedom. And so when we started, we didn't spend a lot of time trying to figure out what was going to be a long-term competitive advantage, whether we were in the right space or not. Just improve that performance. You have to fire a lot of bullets before you fire cannonballs. So firing bullets means what? It means aiming for something and trying to see whether you can hit a target and whether it produces some good results. And a bullet is cheap ammo, of course. So if you fire a lot of bullets, you're going to try a number of things. And in retailing, it's particularly meaningful to try a variety of things. See what works. And once you [have] found something that really works, then you fire the more expensive ammo. So fire a lot of bullets."

"We defined really a strategic framework around reinvigorating the customer experience in retail," Joly said. "It starts with the customers and we had neglected the customers. To do that, we needed to strengthen our team and mobilize the employees around winning again."

Joly immediately instituted a flat management structure while recruiting new outside talent. He pushed out several executive vice presidents and added their duties to a smaller circle of top managers.

"When you think about what we've done with our transformation, we've been able to marry some new talent with mostly existing talent, and then be able to see this culture reignite itself from a focus on the customer," said a senior Best Buy executive. "We got a little carried away with carrying everything, and a little off of our service mission, but we brought in some people. We had a culture of a lot of athletes. Anybody who wanted to be anything got to be it at Best Buy. If I ran stores and I want to run services, I get to. If I was a retailer my entire career and I want to do online, I got to."

"We've had to bring some specialists in," she said. "You can't have everyone as an athlete. But those athletes that are existing in our company have had multiple jobs, they know multiple disciplines, and by sprinkling in some really specific talent, we were able to take this incredible team and transform it."

For instance, Sharon McCollam not only oversaw finances as CFO but also real estate and supply chain as chief administrative officer. Whereas Best Buy used to employ a separate CMO, Joly assigned e-commerce chief Scott Durchslag marketing duties. Shari Ballard, Best Buy's international chief, added human resources and eventually North American stores to her portfolio. To speed up decisions, Joly shrunk Best Buy's corporate bureaucracy from eight business groups to three.

In the past, Best Buy lacked clear command structure to enforce accountability. Turf battles broke out because Best Buy lacked ways to vet ideas and see them through. Good ideas came and went by the wayside.

"Best Buy dabbled in many things but did not take it past the finish line," said Spieckerman, the retail consultant. "They let it die on the vine."

In 2004, Best Buy experimented with "neighborhood boutiques" customized for specific consumer types gleaned from Customer Centricity, including Studio D for "Jill" and Escape for "Buzz." The company even hired Edwin Schlossberg, a famed American designer (and husband of Caroline Kennedy), to design the concept stores.

For soccer moms, the Studio D concept featured classrooms, subtler lighting, and warm, homelike displays to convey a feeling of intimacy. Escape offered an industrial, club-like atmosphere for younger tech enthusiasts. But the idea went nowhere.

When a founder like Schulze leaves the company, things move slower, said former Sony executive Jay Samit.

"That's the advantage of having a founder CEO who has ultimate control of his company," Samit said. "He can make a decision. Right or wrong, but he can make one. A large corporation can't make decisions of that speed. Bill Gates realized one day that he missed out on this thing called the Internet. Microsoft was behind."

"He sent out a memo that's become known as the tsunami memo where he changed the job of one-third of the company worldwide in one memo. It said: 'A third of you are now working on this thing called the Internet. Figure it out.' Do you think some guy that was hired and worked his way up in the company can make those types of changes and have the board back him? Never. The second your founder leaves, a big chunk of that entrepreneurial fire goes with him."

Best Buy could have downsized the high costs of its big-box stores by creating intimate outlets that focused on interactive experiences, much the way Apple has successfully done, said Robin Lewis, CEO of *The Robin Report*, a newsletter that covers the retail industry.

"[They] blew their biggest opportunity ever," Lewis wrote in a blog post. "Apple didn't miss the opportunity, did they?"[7]

Best Buy also suffered from a reliance on outside consultants, particularly Accenture, said the top logistics executive.

"Best Buy outsourced the entire corporate infrastructure," she said. "Outsourcing is not a bad thing if you manage it. Outsourcing is toxic if you don't. We outsourced hiring of Blue Shirts to the consultants. We weren't even picking our people any more. Culturally, do you see how far away that is from what built Best Buy?"

"Leaders that we have brought in today believe that all the answers are in our stores," the executive said. "If you talk to any retailer and they don't mention that to you, you can start writing about their demise. Because once your stores are no longer your focal point, you've probably completely missed the customer point. Joly completely understood that the answers and the future of Best Buy rode in the pockets of our Blue Shirts."

The company recently restructured its field organization to give more autonomy to store managers.

"We built this enormous infrastructure between stores and the corporate headquarters, and all of a sudden, everything that was going to happen in the stores was being done through a corporate function," the executive said. "Millions of e-mails a year going to our stores, 800 pages a month of tasks being assigned to stores. A large amount of bureaucratic obstacles."

"That's not to say there shouldn't be control from the corporate headquarters of a 1,400-store retail infrastructure," she said. "However, when it involves not empowering the store manager, and for the store manager to begin believing that he does not have control over what happens in his stores, you have lost one of your greatest assets. Because those store managers are the heart of Best Buy. We want the stores serving customers, not reading corporate e-mails, not doing corporate tasks."

To focus Best Buy's energies on sales, Joly dispatched a list of non-core businesses that enjoyed funding and prestige under his predecessors: a venture capital unit that bought stakes in emerging technology companies; a joint venture with British mobile phone retailer Carphone Warehouse to develop stores in Europe; and mindSHIFT, a cloud computing firm Best Buy had purchased under Brian Dunn to expand into the small-business market.

In other words, Joly not only simplified Best Buy's corporate structure but also its mission and strategy. He also said the company should hold its executives and rank and file accountable for their performance.

To that effect, during his first week at Best Buy, Joly threw on a blue polo shirt and a name badge that read "CEO-in-Training" and worked the sales floor of a store. Joly also attended the midnight release of the Xbox One and PlayStation 4 at a Best Buy in New York, chatting with customers who waited hours to purchase video game consoles.

"I believe in the well-established concept of the 'servant leader,'" Joly said. "The idea is that the leader of an organization, much like the head of a city, state or country, does not just lead the people around him or her or the institution itself, but acts also as a servant of both. Power is not anointed, and it comes with a responsibility to serve the organization."[8]

Unlike his predecessors, Joly actively courted Wall Street investors, even hosting an Analyst Day just a week after Hurricane Sandy struck New York in November 2012.

"That was the most information we ever got out of the company," one analyst said.

Last year, the board of directors made several changes to its corporate governance practices. First, departing executives are now held to a one-year noncompete period, a standard practice. Second, the company said executives could lose cash and stock for "Voluntary Termination without Good Reason" or "Involuntary Termination with Cause." In other words, in case they quit under pressure or were fired.

Under this scenario, Joly would have had to forfeit $3.7 million, including $2.1 million in cash and $1.6 million in stock. Other top execs, including McCollam and Ballard, would pay back $500,000 apiece.

At the same time, Joly demands accountability from his employees. He ended a controversial program at corporate headquarters called Results Only Workplace Environment (ROWE), which allowed employees to work wherever and whenever they wanted just as long as they completed their projects.

"This program was based on the premise that the right leadership style is always delegation," Joly said. "It operated on the assumption that if an employee's objectives were agreed to, the manager should always delegate to the employee how those objectives were met."

"Well, anyone who has led a team knows that delegation is not always the most effective leadership style," he said. "If you delegate to me the job of building a brick wall, you will be disappointed in the result! Depending on the skill and will of the individual, the right leadership style may be coaching, motivating, or directing rather than delegating. A leader has to pick the right style of leadership for each employee, and it is not one-size-fits-all, as the ROWE program would have suggested."

Joly wants to build a culture at Best Buy bigger than any one individual, even its founder or CEO. He is particularly enamored with *The Fifth Discipline* by management guru Peter Senge at MIT.

"A leader must lead not just for today but also for the future," Joly wrote. "Leaders must keep in mind what legacy they are seeking to build, with an eye toward creating a team to whom they can pass the baton. In the end, any good leader has to be measured in part by what comes after he or she leaves office, which, of course, ties closely to the idea of the leader being dispensable."

"To be clear, I hope and expect that I will have the job of CEO for many years to come but, should my job status change, Best Buy would go on without me. Peter Senge writes that a leader who believes they are their job will inevitably make decisions that are designed to ensure they keep that job. Leaders need to remind themselves that they and their identities are distinct from their position and that they will leave someday, with the organization going on without them. That is why it is so critical that good leaders focus not on preserving their job but serving the organization and preparing the next generation to assume their role."[9]

Though two completely different companies, Target and Best Buy are essentially two sides of the same coin. Both retailers have struggled to balance the desire for innovation, creative thought, and experimentation with the need for operational focus, accountability, and discipline.

Target preferred to develop its own talent because it had supreme confidence in its process and culture. However, that culture encouraged groupthink, which made it hard for employees to offer contrarian ideas. Without fresh perspectives, Target faced a difficult time adapting to the enormous, rapid changes of the digital age because most of its executives were steeped in the company's department store roots, where merchandise and marketing, not technology, took top priority.

As a result, Target recruited outside executives like Jeff Jones to usher in a new culture of experimentation that gave permission to its employees to roll out less than perfect products and fix them on the fly.

Best Buy, on the other hand, indulged the worst excesses of its employees with a decentralized structure that created anarchy rather than innovation. From ROWE and half-baked projects to turf battles and dysfunctional meetings, Best Buy's focus on democracy shifted the balance of power from manager to employee at the expense of speed and accountability.

"This was an organization that had an extraordinary culture for many, many, many years," the top Best Buy executive said. "A winning spirit. A passion for the customer. A belief that knowledge was what you owed a customer in a store. That actually never left Best Buy."

"What started to fade as they became so successful was the diligence in the company around the small things," she said. "Wall Street's asked me 'What are some of the things that have surprised you the most about Best Buy?' One of the things that surprised me the most is the unbelievable talent that they attracted to this company, and the merchandising strength that exists within Best Buy. There's a lot of people that would like our consumer electronics people. The fact that these people have stayed in this culture for so many years, it's amazing to me."

Under Joly, the company flattened its top management ranks and simplified its strategy by divesting businesses not essential to Best Buy's core U.S. store operations. He also ended ROWE, not just for the sake of dragging employees back to work but to rebuild a wayward culture, in which everyone has skin in the game.

"You are seeing people say, 'You know, we used to always do this, I'm so glad to see it again,'" the top logistic executive said. "But it had to be role-modeled by the executives. Our executives have embraced it, and our executives are walking the walk, and talking the talk."

CHAPTER 8

JUMBOTRON

AT&T STADIUM IS BIG.

Not just in physical size but also in concept and attitude. Completed in 2009, the $1.2 billion, 80,000-seat facility in Arlington, Texas, is home to the Dallas Cowboys, a football team not shy about embracing its self-appointed moniker, "America's Team." From Hall of Famers Emmitt Smith and Troy Aikman to larger-than-life billionaire owner Jerry Jones, the Cowboys are big in every sense of the word.

Therefore, the stadium is a perfect monument to that bigness. The glass-enclosed biosphere-like building boasts the world's largest column-free interior and the fourth-largest high-definition video screen, which stretches a staggering 50 yards across the field. The jumbotron is so big that punters have occasionally seen their kicks ricochet off the structure.

On a warm Tuesday in mid-December 2013, Chris Koller stood on a makeshift platform about 100 rows up from the field. He was just about to give a series of interviews to media outlets about Best Buy's Ultimate Showdown, a national championship of sorts for the country's best players of the popular Madden football video game.

It was also a chance for Koller to bathe in the spotlight for a change. As Best Buy's vice president of entertainment, Koller can be considered a black sheep of sorts in the company hierarchy. He oversees the once-dominant but now declining categories that CEO Hubert Joly wants to reduce at stores: CDs, DVDs, and video games.

While new technology like iTunes and Netflix desecrated sales of physical music and movies, it was the lack of new technology that severely hurt video games. At the time, Sony and Microsoft, the makers of PlayStation and Xbox, had not released a new console in seven years. It's no accident that between 2009 and 2012, video game sales dropped about 34 percent to $6.7 billion, according to market research firm NPD Group. Sales of physical games fell 21 percent alone last year compared with 2011.[1]

So when Sony and Microsoft simultaneously debuted PlayStation 4 and Xbox One in late 2013, Best Buy aggressively seized the moment.

"We wanted to take advantage of the excitement around the new consoles, which don't happen very often," a Best Buy gaming executive said. "We thought, 'What could we do to really drive not only the excitement that we know is around there, with but how do we direct people in[to] the store?"

Best Buy has sponsored video game tournaments before. But with the rarity of the near-simultaneous launch of the PlayStation 4 and Xbox One, the company needed to do more: a multistage marketing strategy capped off by a big finale.

The first step was to target hardcore gamers, the first customers likely to buy the consoles. Through its website, texts, and social media, Best Buy encouraged gamers to preorder the consoles, which they could pick up at midnight launch parties around the country.

"The gaming customer wants to have access to information, to be treated fairly, to be transparent with them," the gaming executive said. "So much to the point when we did our launches of Xbox One and PlayStation 4 we sent out FAQs and we posted them online saying, 'This is exactly how we're going to handle the midnight openings, if you have a preorder you're going to go here and you're going to do this. You're going to go in early; you're going to have access to it.'"

Meanwhile, Best Buy reconfigured its store layout to better present the consoles and related games accessories with attractive displays and end caps. For maximum dramatic effect, Microsoft even hired black-and-green armored trucks to deliver the first shipments of Xboxes to Best Buy stores.

"So we've really been focusing on showcasing our technologies, our products on the floor," the executive said. "We've changed all of our gaming departments since the fall, in preparation for these new launches. We are the only retailer that can bring people together for the excitement and the camaraderie and the competition of it. We can bring them together to efficiently get their games at night, or their consoles when it launches."

"We're also there to help people answer questions," he said. "So these first million people that buy the console probably know exactly what they want, they don't need a lot of help. But the next million, and the next million that sell, eventually people are going to ask 'Hey, what's right for me? Is this going to work with my current system? How can I get the most out of this game?' And that's what Best Buy can do. We can answer their questions, we can get their systems installed if their network isn't up to speed. We can get their trade-ins done. We can do all of that one-on-one, face-to-face, in one of our stores. Of course we have online and phone support but our stores are a unique place that can do that for them."

Best Buy hosted eight regional Madden tournaments around the country, which drove enormous crowds to stores. And for the coup de grâce, the company flew the winners to Dallas to compete for a $1,000 gift card. But the real prize was playing the Madden game on the stadium's jumbotron and meeting celebrities like Emmitt Smith and rapper The Game. Best Buy even had the contestants run out of the locker room tunnel to the cheers of the team mascot and two Cowboys cheerleaders.

"We threw off some different ideas and this one just really seemed to stick," the gaming executive said. "It did exactly what we wanted to do, which was drive traffic, drive excitement, and then have some real cool moment at the end. The biggest screen in the world, the biggest HD screen in the world with the first gaming competition ever on that screen, it's also at Best Buy."

BY NATURE OF THEIR ENORMOUS RETAIL footprint and financial muscle, Best Buy and Target have spent considerable money on advertising and marketing, especially large-scale events that capture eyeballs and buzz: concerts, tournaments, celebrity partnerships, fashion shows, shopping parties. Together, the two big-box chains spent over $2 billion in advertising in 2012.

By contrast, Amazon devotes its cash toward technology and distribution operations. While some might see Amazon's model as more cost efficient given its explosive growth, Best Buy and Target enjoy strong relationships with customers. And shopping, after all, is inherently a social and interactive experience. The challenge, though, for big boxes, is to convert more of that ad spend into both physical and digital sales.

"Where the opportunity lies is in driving that connectivity between the stores and online," said Carol Spieckerman of newmarketbuilders. "Target and Best Buy have been a little bit slow, a little bit late to the party on that, but it's obviously now top of mind. They're talking about marketing in terms of making sure that they're offering the myriad options that their competitors are offering."

For Best Buy, building a marketing strategy around price became less effective as Walmart and Amazon lured away shoppers with bigger discounts and innovations like free shipping. So Best Buy in recent years has centered its efforts around services like Geek Squad and the expertise of Blue Shirts. Best Buy will help customers demystify the confusing world of technology and help shoppers find the right products for their needs through one-on-one consultations and weekend tutorials.

However, such marketing strategies don't exactly fire up the crowds the way doorbusters do. In fact, "weekend tutorials" sounds suspiciously like work, something that might appeal to Baby Boomers but not to tech-savvy Millennials who probably know more about the devices than even the Blue Shirts.

When you think about it, Best Buy carries products that are not just experiential but also *fun*: video games, iPads, music, movies, HD televisions. For Best Buy, the key is to focus its efforts not just on the utilitarian nature of its products but also the fun of them. Fun means customers, especially Millennials, are likely to stay longer in the store to play the latest Xbox game or see which color Beats headphones looks cooler with which device and outfit.

"I think the word that comes to mind is 'literalism,'" Spieckerman said. "Best Buy has been very literal about their business in a way that, I think, has taken the fun out of it, or the potential fun out of it. That is to say, 'Oh, well, it is experiential. Look, you can come into a store and literally pick things up and literally test out features and benefits.' That's different from going in and having a really fun experience in the store, to where people say, 'You know what? Let's go down to Best Buy and hang out for a while.'"

CEO Hubert Joly, who also sits on the board of directors of luxury brand Ralph Lauren, wants to infuse that marketing experience into Best Buy.

"Let me tell you that I'm having [an] enormous amount of fun in this business because you're absolutely right. The products are extraordinary and what we can do with them, it's just fabulous," Joly said.

"Think about selling a quarterly subscription to a father and mother to take their kids every Saturday to Best Buy to discover digital photography or how to build a website or how to create maps or play a game," he said. "That would create an amazing, highly emotional engagement for the customer. The stuff we have is so exciting. It builds personal relationships. We have lost that. I think it's an amazing opportunity for us."

"When I joined the company, I was shocked to see how central the Sunday circular still was in the marketing of the company," Joly said. "I have this vision that, like a publisher of books, games, movies, and music, you have to orchestrate product launches in a way that's exciting and fun. The way Ralph Lauren talks to the consumers and creates buzz and excitement is extraordinary. The way Best Buy talks and interacts with the customer has got to be a lot more about this buzz, this curated experience, this orchestration of events that creates excitement."

In other words, be more like Target.

TARGET ALWAYS KNEW HOW TO THROW A PARTY—literally. The retailer decided to throw a fiftieth anniversary celebration not in downtown Minneapolis (as perhaps the Dayton Brothers would have done) but rather at a warehouse in New York City's Chelsea neighborhood.

You would have thought the well-dressed people lined up outside an unmarked industrial building, complete with ropes and earpiece-wearing bouncers, were trying to score an invite to an exclusive VIP club, which, in a way, was true.

Once waved through, attendees entered not a room but an elevator that seemed more like a converted shipping container. Inside, the event space teemed with people, including Naomi Watts, Josh

Groban, and Tony Bennett. Onstage, Alicia Keyes sang "Happy Birthday" moments before dancers dressed as performers from the Moulin Rouge amused the crowd.

For those people not intimately familiar with Target, it might seem strange that the New York glitterati would flock to a party honoring a retailer that sells toilet paper and toothpaste. But that's the marketing genius of Target, a mass discounter that embedded itself in the world of high fashion luxury retail through a combination of spectacle and fantasy.

"When I look at all of the things that make Target different, there's no question [that] the tonality, that attitude, is clearly one of the things that separates Target," said chief marketing officer Jeff Jones. "That is an equity of this brand. Like any great brand manager, you've got to build on those equities, grow them, and protect them so they keep your brand relevant and thriving. Fun is part of Target."

Unlike Best Buy, whose brand was simply a means to an end (the sale), Target's brand is an end unto itself. The company uses its formidable marketing machine to establish an intense bond between retailer and customer. Shoppers are not loyal to any particular brand that Target sells so much as they are loyal to Target itself.

"Where Target has been a real pioneer, and what has set them apart, and also what has fueled their marketing, is that Target is a brand," Spieckerman said. "People today might take that for granted, but that was a very radical concept when Target started pushing toward the concept that [the] retailer would be a brand. There only were a handful of retailers that had ever achieved that status, like Neiman Marcus, or some of the higher-end retailers. People were proud to walk around with those shopping bags, and they had more cachet than the brands that were in them."

"I think Target was the first mass retailer that declared, 'We're going to be the brand, and all the brands that we carry are going to be subjugated to this banner brand,' instead of just being a box that has brands," she said. "It was very influential with retailers that were not mass retailers. It was also influential with their direct competitor Walmart."

Part of Target's mystique is the retailer's ability to give customers something uniquely special. Beginning with collaboration with renowned architect Michael Graves in 1997, the retailer pioneered the concept of partnering with famed designers to create exclusive merchandise for Target customers.

Over the years, Target has introduced collections from major foreign fashion houses (Liberty, Missoni), up-and-coming designers (Jason Wu and Prabal Gurang), and even other retailers (Neiman Marcus). To boost the feeling of exclusivity, Target produces only a small amount of inventory and limits the time consumers can buy the merchandise, usually for a month or so.

In some ways, Target's strategy is somewhat of a contradiction: unique specialness for everyone. Shoppers get access to fashion-forward designers, whose regularly priced work they could not otherwise afford, plus a feeling of exclusivity because Target is the only retailer to carry the merchandise and only for a short period of time.

"Yes, it was absolutely groundbreaking to bring those types of designers to mass shoppers and loyal Target customers,"

Spieckerman said. "Sort of making Target a special club, if you will, where Target shoppers get stuff that other shoppers that are just in it for price, aren't getting. It really created a compelling culture around Target."

"Having that brand equity gave Target the trump card in wooing some of these designers with some really great cachet," she said.

Josie Natori certainly noticed that cachet. Born in the Philippines, Natori, a former top Wall Street investment banker, enjoys a strong reputation for designing Asian-themed lingerie for upscale department stores like Neiman Marcus and Nordstrom. When Target first approached her in 2010, Natori said she thought "it was a great opportunity to expand into a different audience."

"We always have been in the high end," Natori said. "Clearly, the world has changed. Target has been so successful in their other limited-edition collections."[2]

Target is perhaps the only mass retailer that can credibly host fashion shows during New York's Fashion Week. The retailer has built temporary "pop-up" stores in New York and Toronto where consumers can buy merchandise for 24 hours. Celebrities like Jessica Alba and Zoe Saldana have tweeted photos of their new Missoni scarves or Prabal jackets during Target launch parties.

It's all so glamorous—and so within reach of the average consumer.

Over time, Target has expanded its fashion clout into music and film. The retailer is a sponsor of the American Film Institute and, most importantly, the Grammy Awards. Target has struck deals with major music artists like Taylor Swift, Beyoncé, and

Tony Bennett to release exclusive editions of their albums.

Target actually played catch-up to Walmart in music exclusivity. In 2007, Walmart scored perhaps the biggest music deal for retailers: the Eagles agreed to release a special edition of *Long Road Out of Eden*, the band's first studio album in 27 years, exclusively through the mass retailer. A year later, Best Buy won exclusive rights to release Guns N' Roses' *Chinese Democracy* but the album quickly flopped.

"I think it's also quite interesting to look at that interplay between Walmart and Target during those earlier experimental years," Spieckerman said. "The entertainment exclusives, arguably, Walmart took a little bit more of a leadership role there and then Target was like, 'Hey, wait a minute, we've got to have some entertainment. We've got to have music. We've got to have this all tied in. What are we thinking here? Fashion, music, entertainment, they go together. We should own this.'"

Enter Taylor Swift. In 2010, the country superstar, who previously released a Christmas album at Target in 2007, struck a deal with Target to sell an exclusive edition of *Speak Now*, an album that contained bonus tracks and remixes.

Consumers snatched up over 1 million copies in its first week of release, over 30 percent of that total originating from Target shelves.

"We think we helped push her to a million units in the first week," said John Butcher, a top Target executive in charge of entertainment at the time.[3]

In that first week, the retailer moved 360,000 copies, its best showing ever, and 100,000 more than the 'N Sync album.

Just like Target's fashion partnerships, the success of Swift's album gave the retailer power in the music business, an industry hit hard by declining sales of physical CDs.

"What Taylor did for us, she reminded us that the CD can still be a relevant format," Butcher said. "In 2010, after five years of double-digit declines in CD sales nationally, we had our biggest CD in Target's history. That was huge. I had no idea that could be done, to be honest."

"When we look at major new artists when they hit the scene, Target can be an important element to their success," he said. "When we look at established artists, we know they sold very well for many years and when they come back and release a new album, Target can take their album to a new level."

Under Jeff Jones, Target has developed even more sophisticated music programs around individual artists that combine multiple exclusive album editions, commercials, social media, Internet radio, and surprise events.

In 2013, Target created one of the retailer's most successful campaigns of all time: the rollout of the exclusive edition of *The 20/20 Experience*, Justin Timberlake's first album in six years. The innovative campaign, which fused old media with social media, earned Target an eye-popping 2.2 billion media impressions (the number of times content was viewed), an astonishing figure given today's fragmented media landscape.

The campaign began in March with a well-received commercial that ran immediately after Timberlake's performance at the Grammy Awards.

"Not only did Target steal the thunder from Budweiser, who also featured [Timberlake] in its own ad, the commercial came off as more humorous and generally entertaining than Timberlake's own performance that had aired just moments prior," Billboard magazine wrote at the time.

Target later followed up with another commercial in which more than a dozen hardcore J. T. fans, identified by Target through social media, performed his songs only to be surprised by the artist himself. During a launch party sponsored by Target and iHeart-Radio in Los Angeles, Ryan Seacrest's interview with Timberlake was simultaneously broadcast live on Yahoo!, the CW network, and 175 radio stations owned by Clear Channel.

"It was well-executed," said Steven Dennis, a retail consultant and former Neiman Marcus executive. "It generated a lot of positive PR."[4]

For the release of an exclusive edition of *The 20/20 Experience Part II*, Target hosted a surprise concert in a small club in New Jersey for Timberlake, an event that Target also filmed for a commercial. The company did not promote the event except for a few tantalizing hints on Twitter. The concert ultimately generated a tremendous amount of buzz on social media and good feelings toward Target.

Moving forward, Target wants to extend that same exclusivity toward its online operations. For example, the retailer recently introduced Target Ticket, its foray into digital streaming of music and movies. The company can easily introduce an exclusive digital version of *The 20/20 Experience* as it can with CDs.

"Ticket embodies the notion of being able to actually consume content that we already offer our guests physically," said Casey Carl, Target's digital chief. "To do it digitally is something that's been long overdue. Our guest has demanded that of us. We do really well in all things entertainment, whether movies or music or whatever. We have a ton of exclusive and differentiated content, we've never been able to deliver that to our guests other than an extra DVD that you could then download and put on Ultraviolet."

"Our past exclusivity formula really works, but we have a bunch of our guests that are like 'I want that formula, but I want it the way I want it, which is digitally,'" he continued. "More than anything else, that's what Ticket does today. We're just getting started where we can go with this. It's currently a standalone platform but we will soon integrate into Target.com."

"The ability to really consume content on any of your devices and interact with target.com, that's where we want to go with it," Carl said. "Then it's the question of how big do we want to make it. If you drew an ecosystem around the physical and the digital, our market share in entertainment is huge. It's really important to our guests, especially guests with families. We know that physical will slowly go away in our guests' mind, but that's going to take a long time. We've got to deliver both options because we have guests that only want physical—like my mom."

iTunes after all has long offered digital exclusives from its artists, whether extra tracks, digital booklets, videos, or compilations of songs that top artists enjoy. Apple has sponsored music festivals, such as the popular SXSW in Austin, Texas, and then streamed the performances on iTunes.

With its strong ties to musicians and filmmakers, it would not be hard to see Target pursuing similar strategies with Target Ticket.

It's important to see Target's exclusive partnerships not as single campaigns designed to simply sell more clothes and CDs. In fact, Target's exclusive merchandise makes up only a small part of a store's overall inventory. Instead, the partnerships are part of an overall strategy to establish loyalty not to Taylor Swift or Missoni but rather to the Target brand.

Things like Missoni or Justin Timberlake form only one-half of the retailer's ubiquitous "Expect More, Pay Less" motto. Exclusivity rewards its "best customers" who absolutely love Target. But the retailer is also trying to figure out how to use its marketing skills to court the "Pay Less" side of the equation, those customers that care more about price than cachet.

Target has historically focused on getting its best customers to shop more with loyalty programs like REDcard.

Target first conceived of a proprietary "smart" credit card in the early 2000s. Such cards, which generated big profits, had long been a staple at department stores, and Target felt it was upscale enough to warrant a card of its own.

As both retailer and credit source on so many transactions, Target reaped the benefits of both worlds. It collected the interest and late-payment fees from unpaid credit card balances while generating more sales and customer loyalty.

In fiscal 2012, REDcard purchases made up 13.6 percent of Target's sales, compared to 5.9 percent two years before. Kantar Retail estimates that top card users spend an extra $3,000 or more per year. It also sees REDcard holders visiting Target 21 more times a year than other customers.[5]

Since the Great Recession in 2008, Target customers have reduced their visits to Target stores. So far, the company has managed to blunt the impact by getting its best guests, like REDcard members, to buy more stuff per visit. But Target has struggled of late to generate same-store sales even as it still maintains a healthy profit margin.

However, the strategy shows signs of strain. According to research from Kantar Retail, Target's core customers are better off than average shoppers but they are also more sensitive to a weaker economy. About 37 percent of Target customers said they would eat at restaurants less during a recession compared to 32 percent for all shoppers, according to a Kantar survey in 2013. Thirty-four percent reduced spending for "discretionary products" compared to 30 percent of all shoppers, the survey said.[6]

Faced with declining paychecks, these shoppers are more likely to buy less Missoni clothing or Nate Berkus home goods. Exclusivity and brand power, Target's two core strengths, don't matter as much to consumers during tough economic times.

So Target has been recalibrating its marketing message toward cost-conscious consumers. Interestingly enough, despite Target's higher-end reputation, about a third of Target's annual sales, or $23 billion, come from consumers who make less than $50,000 a year.

In other words, Target wants to engage more of its customer base than just its most loyal shoppers who purchase higher-priced items. According to Kantar, the retailer developed a new segmentation model that groups customers into one of these groups: VIPs (most loyal), Enthusiasts, Convenience, Moderates, Occasional Spenders, and Least Engaged.[7]

For Jeff Jones, the question is how to apply Target's cachet to everyday items, like cereal and detergent, that aren't sexy but are crucial to driving more customers to stores on a more frequent basis using tools like REDcard and Cartwheel.

"'Expect More' doesn't always have to be fashion and frivolity," Jones said. "Saving a lot of money, getting a great value, that could be an expectation as well and so that's why we think REDcard and Cartwheel are two examples that bring that value proposition together."

Last year, the company launched a new ad campaign that used runway models to tout its growing grocery line. Target, with ad agency Mono in Minneapolis, created eight tongue-in-cheek TV spots that treat groceries like fashion accessories in a photo shoot. In one spot, a model decked out in a white dress and heels struts through the food aisle while muffin and cake boxes explode in different colors. She then crushes an egg with her hand.

"What we were trying to do was disrupt common convention about how you think about grocery marketing," Jones said. "That campaign was designed to bring fashion and fun to a frequency. It is one of the most memorable campaigns in Target's history."

"We broke lots of new ground socially with the Twitter runway campaign in terms of learning and innovation and experimentation," he said. "We drove meaningful increases in trips among our most loyal guests with that campaign."

This year, Target launched its most ambitious effort to court frequent, price-conscious consumers. The idea is to encourage consumers to load up as much as they can on everyday needs like groceries and household items.

"2013 was the first time we had enough experience to think about running a national grocery campaign," Jones said. "We wanted to bring fashion and fun to frequency. With our new essentials campaign, we want to tell people Target can be a place for quick trips, everyday trips, not just make a list and come on a weekend. Strategically, that's important to the business and so we're going to do two things. One is we're going to feature our iconic hand basket as a symbol of convenience and the entire campaign is going to build on really common vernacular that our guests use called the 'Target Run.'"

For Target, the goal is not just to simply get consumers to purchase more but also to offer suggestions on product combinations they might need. For example, a customer's daughter wants to be a princess for Halloween. So instead of just buying the costume, Target will also encourage the mother to buy candy, a DVD of the movie *Tangled*, and perhaps Advil for the stressed-out mom.

"We'll put together a basket of items," Jones said. "A pet has wandered on to your porch and the daughter wants to keep the pet and you know that's like, 'Mom, can I keep him?' In that case, there might be dog food, a collar, a dog treat, and Zyrtec allergy medicine in the basket."

In short, the campaign wants to highlight Target's bigness, its broad selection of merchandise that consumers can buy in combinations that make the most sense for their needs.

"Just imagine what are all the different kinds of Target Runs that people make, with great combinations of national brands, our own brands, and kind of unexpected combinations of things," Jones said. "That's where the Target weight comes in. It's not just dog food for a low price but it's everything you need to have a great pet. The Target Run we know is common vernacular with people today and we're going to make that a really, really big idea with our essentials campaign."

BEST BUY AND TARGET ARE BOTH BIG BOXES with big marketing budgets. The two companies thrive on creating excitement through event and spectacle, a talent that online retailers like Amazon cannot match. Having a physical presence, a gathering place for likeminded consumers to share mutual passions and experiences, certainly helps.

Think about it this way. Why do you suppose crowds line up outside a Best Buy, Target, or Walmart on Black Friday, even though they can easily get the same merchandise at the same or even lower prices online days or perhaps even weeks before the event? Even more remarkable, the crowds still arrive in force even when most major retailers now hold "Black Friday" sales on Thanksgiving right after turkey dinner.

"I think it says something more about human behavior than it does anything else," Jeff Jones said. "A ritual has been created and that ritual is about going out late on Thursday night and making it a sport, making it a social occasion, making it fun with friends and family to go find the best deals possible. I can't see a day right now when that ritual goes away and so, it's become part of the fabric of shopping in America."

No retailers have arguably exploited spectacle better than Best Buy and Target. Best Buy has largely crafted its brand image around price, hence its name. The company created the Door Buster sales gimmick that's now a staple of nearly every retailer's Black Friday strategy. As for Target, the company has successfully crafted an image of affordable luxury, thanks to stylish, sophisticated marketing campaigns fueled by exclusive partnerships with designers and celebrities in music, television, and films.

But both retailers in recent years have had to adjust their strategies as more consumers have flocked to the Internet and spent less money since the Great Recession. In some cases, Best Buy and Target have borrowed from the other's playbook.

For example, Best Buy suffers from the impression that Amazon and Walmart offer lower prices. Though Best Buy has somewhat blunted that impact by promising to match competitor prices, the retailer knows price alone can no longer drive its core marketing message.

So the company needs new reasons for shoppers to visit its stores. Like Target, Best Buy is focusing on exclusivity through in-store brands like Magnolia and Pacific Kitchen and special partnerships with outside vendors like Samsung and Microsoft.

In the past, Best Buy, like many big-box retailers, focused on muscling vendors for the lowest price. Today, the company is actively working with manufacturers to position Best Buy as the place where consumers can receive both expert advice and fun, especially in categories like video games, mobile devices, and televisions.

"I think Best Buy was somewhat delusional about their customers," Carol Spieckerman said. "Did they really ever have anybody who rallied around the Best Buy brand, or were they just enjoying a certain kind of shopping that happened during a certain era in retail and no longer does?"

Now, instead of dismissing manufacturers as a means to an end, "Best Buy is saying: 'You know what? These brands have the tribes, the loyal fan bases, we're going to become a flagship store for them,'" Spieckerman said. "When you are more important to those brands, brands play ball with you, they take you seriously. For a while anybody that was in consumer electronics had to care about Best Buy, but I don't know if the brands were really pulling for them and advocating for them and paying that kind of extreme attention. I think the stores-within-a-store goes a long way toward where their brand partners are putting their best ideas out there and putting them in a Best Buy store."

As for Target, the retailer has historically distinguished itself from rivals like Walmart by emphasizing perception over price. Tapping into its department store heritage, Target forged an identity more akin to Nordstrom than a mass discounter that sells pet food and bottled water.

But as post–Great Recession consumers cut spending, Target wants to focus on shoppers beyond its best guests by crafting campaigns that appeal to shoppers who appreciate price and value over exclusive design collections. To that end, the retailer's new Target Run campaign emphasizes its large product assortment by encouraging consumers to stock up on groceries and everyday household items each trip, using incentives like REDcard discounts and Cartwheel digital savings.

Perhaps Target's most profound transformation is its most subtle. At Target, the most dominant brand has always been Target. Even when partnering with designers and artists, the company has always taken the lead position in the minds of consumers. Target also prides itself on developing everything in house, from talent and technology to merchandising and marketing. There is a Target Way and then there's everything else.

But as Target's same-store sales have stagnated, the retailer is looking more to the outside. The company says it will now use its considerable financial resources to acquire other brands, something Target has until now avoided. For instance, the company purchased Cooking.com and CHEFS Catalog, two high-end food/kitchen brands with strong online followings and content beyond Target's current capabilities.

"On the chef side, it will really be ingrained within our gift registry experience," Casey Carl said, "so that as a Target customer, you now have access not [only] to all the regular brands in our stores and website, but Le Creuset and Gustav, really high-end brands from CHEFS Catalog."

"The acquisitions are really helping us expand the universe in terms of brands, products, and content. But also, to each of them, we're bringing Target. We're bringing all of our traffic in our stores, on our website, to you. There's a lot more we could do with it, but just bringing those worlds together through our website, in our stores, is going to be a big thing."

CHAPTER 9

VALENTINE'S DAY SURPRISE

AMAZON UPPED THE ANTE—AGAIN.

In late 2013, the Internet giant decided to extend its "Deliver by Christmas" order window until noon on Monday, December 23, an unprecedented (and audacious) move.

The top leadership at Best Buy took notice.

"Amazon did something very, very strategic at holiday and it basically blindsided every retailer in America except Amazon," said the top logistics executive at Best Buy. "I do not know of another retailer that did not cut off sometime on the previous Friday."

However, the crush of holiday packages overwhelmed UPS, Amazon's carrier. And to make matters worse, bad weather struck several regions of the country. The ensuing backlog meant some consumers did not receive their shipments until several days after Christmas.

It was a rare misfire for Amazon, but it also presented an opportunity for Best Buy. While Amazon relies on third-party carriers like UPS, Best Buy can use retail locations from which to ship merchandise directly to consumers. Or even use store staff to deliver packages to homes and businesses.

"You cannot disappoint a customer," the Best Buy executive said. "Amazon did not deliver. This holiday was a fiasco because UPS could not handle the volume over the holidays, and they didn't get those packages delivered."

"That will never happen at Best Buy because we have 1,400 stores shipping," she said. "We, better than they, are going to be in a position to offer the shortest order-to-delivery times in the industry."

Best Buy decided to put this theory to the test. The company announced that it would guarantee Valentine's Day (Friday) deliveries for orders made by 6 p.m. on Thursday.

"We selected a robust assortment of gifts for the customer," the executive said. "We made it all about gifting. We looked at our inventory, we said, 'Are we deep in inventory, can the stores support us if something went wrong?' "

Once again, a major winter storm struck the northeast on Valentine's Day, burying New York and Vermont with snow. Best Buy monitored the status of packages via UPS every 30 minutes and ultimately determined that UPS would not be able to deliver 43 orders. So the retailer had store employees grab products off the shelves and personally deliver them to those customers.

"Our stores were our backup plan," the executive said. "On the orders that UPS could not deliver, we called our stores and said, 'Your job today is to pull this product for Mrs. Jones, and we're going to have someone deliver it to her.' What we're going to say to Mrs. Jones is, 'Mrs. Jones, you ordered this from Best Buy yesterday, we are delivering it. Your package has been delayed because of the weather. I'm from the store, and here it is. When your package arrives, just please send it back to us at your convenience.' One of the Geek Squad agents shows up with his little badge, and he's like, 'Hi, here I am.' "

"When we talk about a maniacal focus on the customer, that is a maniacal focus on the customer," she said. "That is how Best Buy is going to win, and we have the network to do it."

THIS BOOK HAS EXAMINED THE PAST and present of big-box retail through the eyes of Best Buy and Target. Now we look to the future: to see how the two mega-retailers will further leverage their size to not only compete but also thrive in the digital age.

Ironically, the biggest knock on big box is size. Between Best Buy and Target, the two companies operate about 3,000 stores in the United States, each location occupying anywhere from 125,000 to 250,000 square feet.

Running these labor-intensive stores, of course, requires an enormous amount of cash flow. As fewer people visit stores and more shop online, sales per square foot shrink and profit margins decline.

Critics say big-box stores face two choices: close stores or get more people to shop at them. But neither option on its own is particularly viable. Closing stores may save money in the short term but still does not solve the core problem of how to increase sales. Big box should of course attract more people to stores but the format will probably never draw the same crowds as it did before the Internet.

And certainly not after the Great Recession in 2008, as consumers continue to reduce spending.

"There is a finite amount of money that households have to spend on what they buy from retailers and more retailers are offering roughly comparable things," said Keith Anderson from RetailNet Group. "That means somebody's going to win and somebody's going to lose."

For big boxes, the solution is not simply looking at stores as standalone assets but rather as the key component in a hybrid digital/physical distribution system in which goods and services flow seamlessly to the customer where and when they want them.

"This is the model of the future," said Gerald Storch, the former top executive at Target and Toys "R" Us. "Over history it's been called multichannel, it's been bricks and clicks. Ultimately the winning formula is one where the stores, the Internet, mobile, this is how we all interact with everything. All work as one for the customer. Here we are in a physical location. Physicality has many inherent advantages certainly. You go to bricks and mortar as you go to the movies. It's instant plus you can say, 'Oh look at those greeting cards.' They have texture, they're not just pictures."

"Even Amazon will need to become physical to succeed in the future," Storch said. "Every chain of stores has hundreds or thousands of distribution points. The issue is repurposing those stores so they can function not just as traditional retail stores but also as showrooms and as Internet distribution points."

Gap Inc. in particular has aggressively positioned its stores at the center of its omnichannel universe. In addition to ship-from-store, the specialty clothing retailer also offers "reserve-in-store," which allows consumers to set aside clothing in certain sizes and styles prior to visiting the store.

"Reserve-in-store addresses one of the age-old issues associated with the perils of shopping," said Art Peck, president of growth, innovation, and digital at Gap. "Which is when I go into the store, I drive my car to mall, I find a parking place, I walk into the mall, I go down to the aisle, I walk into the store and I shop. It's really frustrating when you find that pair of jeans that you want and that amazing wash but your size isn't there. What reserve-in-store is, is simply the way for a customer with confidence to go into our stores and know that the thing that they want to buy is going to be there."

"Now you might say, why can't you just order online then go to the store and pick it up?" he said. "Frankly our products are not inherently objective. I mean they fit differently, you want to touch them; you want to see what the color is. It's not like buying a toaster or book or something like that."

Gap will also allow consumers to order merchandise within the store. A customer who can't find the right size or style can scan an item with a smartphone and the retailer will ship it to the store or the consumer's home.

"It just gives you that much more confidence that when you go into a store you're not going to leave empty-handed, and for the industry that is a big deal," Peck said. "For us it's a big opportunity we think, to create a different in-store experience. Give the customer that confidence that any time they go into the store, they're going to have a successful shopping experience."

If there's one thing Best Buy did right, it picked great locations for its stores. About 70 percent of the population in the United States lives within 15 minutes of a Best Buy. The proximity to customers allows each store to act as a mini distribution center where consumers can pick up merchandise or have the stores deliver to their homes and workplaces.

As Best Buy envisions and has experimented with—as seen with its Valentine's Day delivery system—each store can hire a courier or have an employee personally walk that iPhone to someone's front door.

But even with free shipping, about a third of Best Buy customers choose to pick up orders in store. About 40 percent of Best Buy's annual revenue comes from those products.

"Explain that," said the top logistics executive. "They want it their way. They want it how, when, and where they want it. No matter what Amazon does, the company can't fully meet customers' needs unless they decide to enter the store business."

Big-box companies may also find some help in Silicon Valley. A number of startups are working on ways to help retailers better deliver products to consumers and stock shelves with more differentiated merchandise.

Storefront, a startup in San Francisco, is talking to national retailers about using its software to rent out shelf space or even whole sections of the store to unknown merchants selling unique products.

"We see in the not too distant future the best merchandise financed by Kickstarter campaigns at Best Buy," said founder and CEO Erik Eliason. "So you can try the products in the store. We see the experience being very valuable at Best Buy."

Instacart, funded by high-powered venture capital firms like Khosla Ventures and Andreessen Horowitz, created a mobile app that allows one-hour delivery of groceries to online customers in San Francisco, Chicago, and New York. Under the San Francisco–based company's model, Instacart hires "personal shoppers" to buy the merchandise at the store and deliver them to consumers. To fit a one-hour delivery window, the company's software identifies the right shopper and store location based on factors like weather, time of day, and traffic.

Instacart founder Apoorva Mehta, a former software engineer at Amazon, said he wants to expand the service to all retailers.

So in theory, a personal shopper could deliver a television or a sweater from a Best Buy and Target store to an online customer in just 60 minutes, something that Amazon can't do—yet.

"We want every single retailer to be on this platform because we have data to show them that we're bringing them new customers and larger order sizes," Mehta said. "We're providing them essentially with a new store but no extra fixed cost associated with it."

"That's a very powerful way to think about the future," he said. "Anything that can become on-demand will become on-demand. If you look over a five- to ten-year horizon, people are going to want faster deliveries and more selection. It's not just shipping the products next day or two days. It's now. And that's just not possible if you're an Amazon and operate warehouses and delivery trucks."

Amazon is well aware of its limitations. The company is reportedly looking to open physical stores. And the company is aggressively exploring drones that can bypass UPS altogether and directly deliver products from a warehouse to a home or business.

If Amazon succeeds, big-box retailers might follow suit.

"If you do research, I think you will find that one of the largest individual investors in robotics technologies is Jeff Bezos," the top logistics executive at Best Buy said. "Jeff Bezos did not talk about drones to look like a crazy person. He obviously has something in beta today that he believes is going to work, or somebody's got it on a drawing table in one of the companies where he's a big investor."

"We ourselves are looking at the various technologies that exist," she said. "I promise you that with our obsession over the customer experience and how quickly we can deliver, if a drone is necessary to do that, we will not be last in line like we were with the online channel."

If an integrated bricks-and-clicks model represents the future, then data is the lubricant that will slide the pieces together. And no one sits on more data than big-box retailers like Best Buy and Target.

"This is the Holy Grail, because there are companies with multibillion dollar valuations sitting in Silicon Valley," said the

Best Buy executive, "and the only reason that they have a valuation at all is because they have the ability to know your customer, and socialize, and be able to make things relevant."

"Data is probably the most valuable asset in Best Buy," she said. "In this day and age, real estate and DCs [distribution centers] are only important to the extent you can bring customers to the brand. I believe that my stores are more powerful when I can have relevant reasons for you to come to one. We have one of the largest house files in the country, probably in the world, to be honest, and we do nothing with it."

For example, Best Buy still primarily relies on generic e-mails and Sunday newspaper circulars.

"People do not want blast e-mail," the executive said. "That's all we're doing. Yet, we have more customer data in Best Buy than probably, I would say, 95 percent of most retailers, because of our scale. It resides in hundreds of databases."

Big Data offers a number of possibilities, including the idea that retailers can adjust prices in real time depending on the individual consumer, said former Sony executive Jay Samit.

"If it wasn't for sky marshals being armed, I want to walk up and down the aisle of a plane and ask each person on the plane what they paid for a ticket," Samit said. "I believe no two people pay the same price because airlines are using Big Data to do dynamic pricing on each ticket."

"Would we agree that is probably the best way that every product should be priced?" he said. "A restaurant should have been half off today because they've got a full hotel and nobody's coming."

"Retail will be the same way," Samit said. "Every product will communicate to me into my environment and know who I am, so you and I are shopping the supermarket together. You bought Pampers last week. I bought Luvs. Pampers is going to give me a coupon to try to switch me but not you. That's smart business. Putting a coupon in the newspaper, the old way, when you religiously bought Pampers for 20 years, and you're now giving me a dollar off? You're just throwing away margin."

Combing through customer data to spot patterns and predict future behavior is not a new concept. The question for retailers is how to best exploit the information to generate sales and earn customer loyalty.

"That technology all exists today," Samit said. "It's not more expensive for the retailer, but it's listening to Big Data and looking at your IT department as a profit center and not a cost center. The strategy is there. None of this is like, 'Holy crap.'"

Take the smartphone. Retailers have long dreamed of a technology that could interact with store customers as they shopped in real time. In the early 2000s, the buzz centered around radio-frequency identification (RFID) tags implanted on products. Companies could track inventories throughout the supply chain by reading each tag's unique electromagnetic signature. The same technology, same thought, could be applied to consumers who had RFID tags on their person. Retailers could monitor the exchange of information between RFID tags on the customer and the merchandise.

A few years later, high-end retailers like Estée Lauder and Macy's equipped their employees with special iPads that could help them communicate with foreign customers.

"If a consumer comes up and they don't speak English, associates can easily access their language along with the English translation on the tablet," said Maya Mikhailov, co-founder of GPShopper, which designed the software for the iPad. "Instead of pointing and gesturing, employee and customer could have this interactive experience they couldn't possibly have had before. In New York, the Estée Lauder iPads are in all the flagship locations and Macy's has four of them. There are more and more people all around the world traveling, they speak all sorts of different languages and they wish to engage."

But Mikhailov admits technologies like RFID were missing the point because they were primarily designed for employees, not customers. With the growing dominance of smartphones, the next step was to design software that would empower consumers to interact with the store.

In 2013, Apple debuted iBeacon as part of its new iOS 7 mobile operating system. iBeacon, an indoor positioning system consisting of low-cost transmitters, can alert iPhones to other iPhones in the area and transmit information between the devices via Bluetooth.

Mikhailov believes iBeacon will transform retail. For one thing, iPhones, along with Androids, are so wildly popular, they have become the de facto technology standard for retailers to reach consumers.

"We're very excited about the beacons," she said. "What makes beacons really exciting is not just the hardware of the beacon itself but Apple. Everybody who's downloaded iOS 7 automatically has Bluetooth turned on in their device. Apple threw a stake in the ground. With all of these different technologies like RFID to get people more engaged in the stores, people were wondering, 'What's the next in-store engagement?' Then Apple quietly said: 'We support this one.' Now retailers can use iBeacon with[in] the four walls of their stores to offer consumers super-personalized and super-contextualized experiences."

"Take Walmart. When you get near a particular store, Walmart's GPS-based smartphone app says, 'Would you like to switch on in-store mode?' " Mikhailov said. "If the consumer says yes, it really reforms the mobile application to make it the remote control for this particular location. If you're in the grocery section the app can just flip to recipes because it recognizes that you're in the grocery section. If you walk to the consumer electronics section and start dwelling there, all of a sudden the app can flip to give you more information on the latest gadgets that are coming out."

Other industries have started to embrace the technology. Major League Baseball recently rolled out an app that uses iBeacon to send information to fans on their smartphones as soon they walk into the stadium. For now, baseball plans to use iBeacon just for checking in fans. In the future, though, teams could provide discounts on merchandise and tickets, a chance to upgrade seats, or watch batting practice on the field.

Target is exploring a different location-based technology. The retailer partnered with IndoorAtlas, a startup that developed an indoor GPS system that mimics migratory animals who can navigate home without ever getting lost. The technology relies on the built-in compasses, or manometers, in smartphones to detect anomalies in the Earth's geomagnetic field. Based on this data, the system can guide users through indoor spaces and detect objects within six feet of their actual location.

"IndoorAtlas technology bypasses Wi-Fi, Bluetooth beacons, and GPS," said CEO and founder Janne Haverinen. "This opens up a world of possibilities for in-store and in-mall mapping mobile apps that support location-based point-of-sale, advertising, and marketing."[1]

Thanks to these even smarter smartphones, retailers can finally start to put customer data they collect to novel use. Best Buy launched "Project Athena," an ambitious attempt to mine its vast hoard of data and build better customer profiles each time it adds more information.

"Athena is the goddess of wisdom, of course, but the name was given to it because it's the wisdom of all things related to our customers, and every day it gets better," the Best Buy logistics executive said.

"Think about this," she said. "Today, let's say I marry Geek Squad with My Best Buy loyalty, and then I marry the next thing. Every time I talk to you, I'm getting more relevant. But every day, every week, every month, you just keep adding, and you become more and more and more real, and we become more and more relevant."

Eventually, Best Buy envisions crafting holistic "grids" in which the retailer can customize itself to consumers based on a constant stream of information like purchase histories and social media content. In effect, customers become living, breathing algorithms—mathematical models that Best Buy constantly refine with more data.

"I've thought a lot about it," said the Best Buy e-commerce executive. "We're going to first integrate all of the data we have on our customers over the last 15 years. It's been sitting in seven different databases completely siloed and inaccessible to each other. We are then able to take a 360-degree view of the customer, just based on what they've done with us over the last decade. That's step number one."

"We then link this data into Twitter, into Pinterest," he said. "Since I have your unique identifier through My Best Buy, with your permission, I can now start to link in information from social media accounts. In return for you giving me that permission, I promise to give you radically relevant recommendations about the things you care about most."

"I want to build a product grid, which only we have. We know what products are coming out when, from which vendors," he said. "We know who's got the highest reviews, we know who's got the best return rates, we know where there's warranty problems. We've got a goldmine of information that any manufacturer would kill to have about their products, that they don't even have about their own stuff. I can bring those four things together into a set of different experiences, in a way that nobody else possibly can, not even Amazon."

So what does this vision look like in the real world?

"You've signed up for My Best Buy and you have opted in for Geek Squad to come out and do a consultation at your home," the e-commerce executive said. "They come out to your house and they see you're an Apple guy, you've got N Class Wi-Fi, you've got 65-inch LED TVs. They solved a problem you were having with the new PlayStation 4 that you just got hooked up. We know all of this from that one Geek Squad visit. That's now accessible [through] your own personal consumer electronics vault."

"Let's imagine that your house got wiped out by a hurricane the next day," he said. "What are you going to do? Guess what? Because you're a My Best Buy member, we did a deal with your insurance company. That vault that I described is actually proof of purchase as far as they're concerned about replacing everything, all the electronics that you bought with us in your house. In fact, Best Buy will make sure that they're all delivered when and where you want."

"You don't have a job because everything's wiped out, so what are you going to do with your time?" the e-commerce executive said. "We know all of the cool new games and the cool technology that you bought at Best Buy. Your family and friends are able to see the things that you need and what you already own, and what you want."

"We're able to tap into your interest grid and we know that you're into Civil War reenactments," he said. "Based on that, we're able to push recommendations to your phone, almost like a stock ticker, of offers that will let you be able to indulge those interests or passions. Or be able to connect with other people in the Best Buy community who have those interests or passions. We reserve for you the PlayStation 5 with this amazing Civil War game. Everybody else is going to have to wait a week to get that, but because you're a My Best Buy Elite Plus member, the console will be sent to you on the day of the release."

"When you start talking those types of two-, three-, four-level personalizations, you need that 360-degree view," the e-commerce executive said. "Amazon has a relatively static view. I mean, I'm sorry, Prime is cool, it was an amazing idea in its time. But My Best Buy is way beyond what Prime can do. My Best Buy has gone 3.0 and it involves more than just free shipping."

As the executive noted, the key to the future is convincing customers to grant retailers permission to collect and analyze all this data. For today's consumers, that may be a tough sell, given recent data breaches at companies like Target and Neiman Marcus, in which hackers stole personal information from over 100 million customers.

That's why Millennials figure so prominently in the plans of retailers, not just because of their sheer size and buying power but also the generation's natural ease and comfort level with technology, social media, and data use.

Studies show younger consumers are less likely to worry about data and privacy issues than older consumers. In the United States, 59 percent of consumers between ages 18 and 29 worry about data privacy compared with 71 percent of consumers between ages 45 and 60, according to a recent survey by SDL.[2]

Millennials spend about $200 billion a year but, perhaps more importantly, are 2.5 times more likely to be an early adopter of technology than older generations, a study by Barkley marketing firm and Boston Consulting Group says.

Fifty-six percent of Millennials report that they are usually either one of the very first to try new technologies or are among the first group to try a new technology. By contrast, 35 percent of non-Millennials will wait a year before trying a new technology and 22 percent admit that they wait until a technology has become mainstream and well-established before they take the leap.

"When it comes to using the Web, Millennials are 'always on,'" the Barkley/BCG report said. "Their access to multiple Web-enabled devices, at home and on the go, makes them power users of the Internet."[3]

In other words, this generation is more likely to buy into retailers' vision of a data-driven marketplace where these consumers use mobile devices and social media to shop both online *and* in the store.

Contrary to popular belief, Millennials are not exclusive Internet consumers, and many prefer to, and do, visit physical stores for service and selection.

"I actually like to support the brick-and-mortar stores and the expertise of the people at the stores," said Jared Obstfeld, 29, of Denver. "I find value in that. Sometimes I'll get on bestbuy.com to do some research to educate myself but I would never actually buy something like a camera online."

"For me to buy something online, it would have to be something very specific, something that is only found online," he said. "Online, you can't feel how it feels in your hand, how it sounds when you press the buttons, how the jeans fit. It just gives you an opportunity to give it a test run before you commit to buying it."

Tara Miller, 19, of Maple Grove, Minnesota, shops about two to three times a week at Target and Walmart and once every two weeks at Sam's Club. She mainly shops for household necessities and toiletries as well as food and entertainment like movies.

"I like that those big boxes are convenient, and the stores are really well organized so that you can get whatever you need all in a specific area," Miller said. "And it's nice to be able to ask the workers questions about products. I look for price first and then think about how helpful employees are because if they're really good, it makes me want to go back. Same with product quality; if I'm satisfied with the product quality I'll be more likely to return."

To win over these Millennials, retailers are focusing on a device that is essential to these consumers: the smartphone. Sixty percent of Millennials say it's a real convenience to have a smartphone to research or purchase a product or service on the go. More than 50 percent use their smartphones to research products or services while shopping.

"The difference between non-Millennials and Millennials is not whether they conduct research prior to making purchases, or even what resources they utilize," the Barkley/BCG report said. "It's how they conduct it. For Millennials, consumer research isn't done sitting at a desk. Millennials have their smartphones and other mobile devices handy, and they may very well be making their final purchase decisions while standing inside your store comparing prices or determining the origin of a particular product."[4]

For retailers, the key is to use the device to create unique in-store experiences that resonate with these younger consumers.

"The unfortunate reality is most of the people using a smartphone in stores today are either using it to distract their kids so that the shopping trip is a little bit less of a nuisance," said retail consultant Keith Anderson. "Or they're using it to look for a better price on the same thing somewhere else. There are unquestionably loyalty and retention opportunities to transform the cash register in the front end from a cost center and a source of customer frustration to a convenience and a source of customer loyalty."

Collette Forsyth, 22, of Minneapolis says the daily e-mails she receives from Forever 21 don't resonate with her.

"If retailers put as much advertising effort into in-store stuff, and offer enticing deals, I'd be more likely to buy from there," she said.

For example, Best Buy hopes its Reward Zone loyalty program will drive smartphone-savvy Millennials to the stores.

Best Buy hopes to communicate real-time messages to consumers through their smartphones, based on the products they are looking at and how long they linger in a particular section.

"That's the future of omnichannel," said the Best Buy e-commerce executive.

For Target, loyalty also plays a pivotal role in pushing Millennials into the store. Over 50 percent of the 5 million customers who used Target's Cartwheel digital savings app in 2013 were Millennials.

"We're also pleased with the continued growth of Cartwheel," said Kathy Tesija, Target's executive vice president of merchandising. "Younger guests are particularly engaged by Cartwheel, a much higher percentage than they represent in our overall guest base."[5]

The number of Cartwheel users redeeming deals was more than ten times higher than traditional marketing tools like e-mail blasts. The retailer's pre–Black Friday deals on Cartwheel drove one-third of active users into Target stores on the Wednesday before Thanksgiving.

"The smartphone is the portal to the Target universe," said Target digital chief Casey Carl. "It's Target in your pocket at all times. Everything Target will be accessible through the phone at any time. Yeah, mobile is the future."

Encouraged by this success, Target recently added the ability for consumers to scan barcodes to find out if there's a Cartwheel deal on an item. The company also added the capability to sign up for Cartwheel directly through a Target REDcard account and e-mail.

Target is also developing image-recognition technology with which a shopper can take a photo of a product with a smartphone and instantly receive a link to purchase the item. Or the person's own image can be used as a security key to authorize purchases by smartphone.

One intriguing smartphone technology called "augmented reality" would allow the consumer to visualize how merchandise would look in a home prior to a purchase. The consumer can place images of products inside a digital living room or dining room.

"You can literally see, does it look good on this wall, or do I want to bring it over here?" Carl said. "We actually did this at my own house with an ottoman. We were like, 'Should we put it by this sofa or by the chair?' And you're like 'Oh, you're doing this and this? OK, great!' Click it and buy it. Or: 'Nah, none of them, I don't like it at all, let's go to the next one.'"

"Now imagine a world where you're an incoming freshman and we send out a back-to-college catalog to your home," he said. "You see everything we could possibly decorate your dorm with, you could see what that all looks like together without ever buying it."

"Now, is my mom going to use this?" Carl said. "No, she won't know how to use that yet. But it's just one of many things that help us, it's a means to an end. It's how you can experience it better than you could've before. A printed piece of paper, that's good. I can show you that but better. Then if you come to our stores you can see a lot of it, touch it. We're just making that experience better."

Best Buy and Target also want to play to Millennials' interest in social issues, such as the environment and poverty.

"Affiliation with a cause is more important to the Millennial generation than to any previous generation," the Barkley/BCG report said. "Millennials who care about causes are more likely than older generations to show a preference towards companies that support causes—even it means paying a bit more for those companies' products."[6]

A growing number of retailers are trying to fuse commerce with charity. Through its RED initiative, Irish rock band U2 has partnered with Apple, Gap, and Nike to help fund efforts to eliminate AIDS in Africa. Toms Shoes donates a pair of shoes to a child in need for every pair of shoes it sells online and at stores.

Philanthropy aside, charitable projects can translate into good business, especially among retailers. A report by IHL Consulting Group said 65 percent of the consumers it surveyed said they were more likely to shop at a particular retailer if the retailer worked with a charity.

"In a period of retail history that is increasingly defined by a lack of loyalty among customers…there is an opportunity for retailers to connect with their customers by tying themselves to visible and public charitable giving," the report said. "Customers want to know their purchases are making a difference in the world, not just lining the pockets of management and shareholders."[7]

Best Buy hopes Millennials will take a kind eye toward the retailer's extensive electronics recycling and trade-in programs.

"We will have recycled a billion pounds by the end of this year," said the top logistics executive. "People can bring anything they want to a Best Buy store, and all of that would have been in the landfills had we not done it. We never did any marketing with it. We never made that a statement about why I care about the causes you care about, which is the bigger world."

"Trade-in is another thing that we have that we don't make a big statement about," she said. "You're a student, you're a Millennial, you're just starting your career. If I bought a smartphone,

I want it to be worth something. So we're going to allow them to exchange the device for another smartphone and then we're going to recycle the old phone."

"Millennials are very focused on not throwing things away," she said. "I can't believe how many of my nephews told me not to throw away batteries. And all my nephews have these little bags in their rooms. I'm like, 'What is this?' They're like, 'You can't throw away a battery!'"

"Millennials care about causes," the executive said. "In the consumer research that I had tracked for 15 years, it used to be acquisitions of things that was most important to people. Now it has become 'The causes I contribute to.'"

As for Target, the retailer in 2013 applied its exclusive design partnerships to a campaign against hunger.

The company partnered with Lauren Bush Lauren on a collection of clothes, stationery, and home goods to help fund FEED Projects, an organization she founded to combat global hunger. FEED USA + Target featured 50 products priced from $3 to $400. Target donated 10 percent of each sold item's retail price to FEED Projects.

Target also says the collection has the potential to fund more than 10 million meals. The retailer calculates that $1 will equal eight meals, meaning Target projected FEED USA + Target would generate roughly $12.5 million in sales.

Lauren, a fashion model and designer, is the daughter of Neil Bush, brother of George W. Bush and former Florida governor Jeb Bush. She is married to David Lauren, the son of famed fashion mogul Ralph Lauren.

The initiative is a way "to bring our guests a collection founded on great design as well as a cause that may be important to them," said a Target spokeswoman.[8]

This isn't the first time Target has mixed retail with charity and progressive causes. The company has offered Earth Day–related products as well as cards for same-sex couples. Target has also sold some limited-edition holiday-themed Bullseye stuffed animals to benefit St. Jude Children's Research Hospital in Memphis.

But FEED USA represents one of Target's largest social campaigns to date.

Judith Russell, an analyst with *The Robin Report*, an industry newsletter, said FEED USA + Target can help attract young, socially conscious shoppers to Target's stores. At the same time, the prospect of funding a good cause can prompt consumers to open their wallets at a time when money is still tight.

"In times of economic distress, the collection gives us a good excuse to go shopping," Russell said.

One puzzle retailers would dearly love to crack is social media. Millennials prodigiously use Facebook, Twitter, and Pinterest, but so far only to communicate and entertain themselves. Unlike websites, consumers have not yet tapped social networks for commerce.

"I wouldn't think of social media as a professional way of shopping," said Tyler Page, 22, of Minneapolis. "I find that kind of sketchy."

But there is great potential. Research shows that Millennials tend to make decisions collaboratively, often relying on peers for advice and affirmation.

Seventy percent of these consumers said they feel more excited if friends support their plans compared to 48 percent of older Americans. Another 68 percent of Millennials said they make decisions only after consulting with a few people they trust versus 52 percent of older Americans.

Gaining peer approval is crucial because Millennials also distrust anything too commercial. The biggest obstacle to social commerce is the perception of authenticity, said Brian Kelly, a retail consultant and former executive at Sears.

The demographic likely to drive s-commerce would be Millennials such as college students, who are naturally skeptical of any event that is overtly commercial.

"What's the digital equivalent to talking over the back-yard fence to a neighbor?" Kelly said.[9]

So big-box retailers like Best Buy and Target are exploring ways to use their sizable social media audience not only to influence Millennials but to generate sales without offending them.

"You have to educate the buyer on how this is going to help them solve a problem or achieve a goal and really genuinely be useful to your potential customers," said Jill Rowley, a San Francisco–based sales consultant who specializes in social media. "Businesses are built on profitable revenue. So I think the customer knows the goal is to earn their business. The method to earn their business is to provide authentic access to information and people who have used the product."

"If anything starts to become scripted or what I call modern trickery, you will lose that customer for life," she said. "At the end of the sessions, why shouldn't Best Buy give me a channel to make a purchase? Why shouldn't Target make it easy, frictionless, for the customer to make a purchase? They should. But if you do it like, 'You won't get back to the next session unless you buy something from this session,' then you've really offended the buyer. The buyer wants to buy when she is ready, and she is ready when you've provided her enough information that she is going to understand the value she is going to get from the purchase."

Best Buy is an industry leader in using social media as a customer service tool to answer questions and respond to complaints. Using sophisticated software that can monitor more than 200 million sites a day, Best Buy can detect and respond to customer questions or complaints 24 hours a day, seven days a week.

A recent study of the top 100 retailers by Conversocial consulting firm determined Best Buy's average response time to social media queries was 14 minutes compared to an average industry time of 11 hours and 15 minutes. In fact, Conversocial rated Best Buy No. 1 in social customer service, the only retailer to receive its highest rank of five stars.[10]

Best Buy has built an internal Google-like search engine from which employees can quickly access information and answer customer questions. Best Buy is also collecting customer questions and the company's answers so that it can develop content to share with consumers online in the form of videos and blog posts.

Best Buy now wants to apply that social media expertise not just to fix problems and soothe angry customers but to proactively encourage them to buy things.

Last December, the retailer hosted an event on Google Hangouts, an online video chat service of Google Inc. in which customers could talk with Best Buy tech experts about last-minute gift ideas. Shoppers could also buy the products being discussed.

"Over the past few years, we have used social media to amplify our message," said Scott Moore, Best Buy's senior vice president of marketing and a former chief marketing officer for Best Buy Mobile. "Now the biggest opportunity is to drive engagement—to get people to acquire products."

With the Shoppable Hangout, Moore said he hopes the presence of Best Buy's Blue Shirts and Geek Squad agents would especially attract Millennials looking for informative, neutral advice on products.

"What we are looking for is real authenticity," Moore said.[11]

The effort was reminiscent of Target's Bullseye University, the makeshift dormitory set in Los Angeles from which the company live-streamed a group of YouTube personalities hanging out.

In many ways, Bullseye University represented both the promise and limitations of such social media experiments. While Target officials were pleased with the traffic the site attracted, sales were somewhat lacking. Relatively few products were available for sale and technical issues slowed down functionality.

But if retailers can figure it out, the payoff would be significant.

"Right now, a lot of analysts look at social shopping and think, 'Oh this is going nowhere,'" said Toronto-based retail consultant Doug Stephens. "It's a tiny fraction of online retail and within that, it's an even smaller fraction of total retail. But I don't think you can deny the idea that if you have a billion people on Facebook, there's potential to create a marketplace there. Retailers and consumers are still in a bit of an awkward state right now about our relative comfort level with that shopping within the social experience. But in my opinion, it's inevitable."

Making it easy to purchase over Facebook and Twitter "would make me impulse-buy things more," shopper Collette Forsyth said. "It would be almost too convenient."

It makes intuitive sense that the future of big-box retail, indeed of all retail, lies with the Millennial generation. For all of the grand visions of Big Data, smartphones, and omnichannel models, Best Buy and Target need customers to buy into these ideas.

Compared to Baby Boomers and Gen Xers, Millennials embrace mobile devices and social media not as a luxury but rather an integral part of their daily lives. Millennials care about data privacy but are less concerned with security risks compared to older Americans. That's crucial since retailers require customers to voluntarily share their data in order to use that information to influence their shopping behaviors.

Social media, however, remains the biggest prize. Millennials spend an enormous amount of time on Facebook, Twitter, and Instagram. Retailers like Target and Best Buy are trying to figure out ways to prompt these younger consumers to purchase merchandise over social media but without appearing too commercial. Since Millennials rely on advice and support from peers, retailers can generate big sales through social media should they figure out the right balance between education and commerce.

CONCLUSION

BIG IS BETTER

JUST A FEW MONTHS AWAY FROM BLACK FRIDAY 2013, BEST BUY CEO Hubert Joly was in an exceedingly good mood. Under his watch, the company's shares had more than tripled to over $40 a share. During the previous year's holiday shopping season, Best Buy generated flat same-store sales, a remarkable feat for a company that was in quick free fall.

Now Joly wanted more. Given the upcoming release of the new PlayStation 4 and Xbox One and Best Buy's aggressive price plan, Joly was expecting a significant positive comp.

"Flat is *not* the new black," he told a meeting of store and general managers.[1]

Unfortunately for Best Buy, reality struck. Walmart and Amazon cut their prices earlier and steeper than anyone expected. The rest of the industry followed suit.

As a result, even though Best Buy gained market share, the company's same-store sales actually fell 0.9 percent. Best Buy's stock promptly plummeted 30 percent that day as critics once again renewed talk of a Circuit City–like bankruptcy.

It was a sobering moment for the normally upbeat Joly. But it also reminded the turnaround specialist that turnarounds took time and he would inevitably encounter turbulence.

"I was depressed for about 30 minutes about it," Joly said. "But then you recharge the batteries. We asked ourselves: 'Does it change our strategy and our direction?' The answer was no. Everything we're working on makes sense. We just have to work harder and faster. As a leadership team, we went in together and said: 'How are we going to show up? How are we going to behave? Why do we fall?' Isn't that the question that is asked [of] Bruce Wayne in the movie *Batman Begins*? So that we can pick ourselves up. So when you have a competitor like Amazon, a competitor like Costco, a competitor like Walmart, you cannot rest on the laurels that you don't yet have."

"It's a multiyear journey," he said. "So you need to maintain the rhythm. And so one of the things that you have to do in a turnaround is that even if the share price goes down, like ours did in January, you have to emphasize the wins, including the small wins."[2]

Target has also been humbled by its own missteps and the vast changes in the retail industry. Same-store sales have been declining. The company fumbled its much anticipated entry into Canada, a country where consumers already liked the Target brand. And in December 2013, in the midst of the key holiday shopping season, Target disclosed that hackers had stolen personal data from millions of customers.

As a result, Target has undergone sweeping changes to its culture. In May 2014, for the first time in its history, the company fired its CEO, Gregg Steinhafel. Also for the first time, Target hired an outsider to replace him. Brian Cornell, a former top executive at Safeway and PepsiCo, now must lead Target through perhaps the most challenging time in the company's history.

Complicating matters is Wall Street. For even as it punishes Best Buy and Target stock, it rewards Amazon, which despite its frothy sales growth does not make much, if any, profit from retail. Unlimited free shipping and perpetually low prices do cost money.

"Amazon does not make money but yet the company has this giant $100 million market cap," said Gerald Storch, the former CEO of Toys "R" Us and vice chairman at Target. "It's all based on the company's future. Whereas the bricks-and-mortar retailer has to match Amazon today on price and on shipping and earn less on the Internet sales today than they do on bricks-and-mortar sales. They get punished by the Street for not making their earnings. Traditional retailers can't defend themselves saying 'Whoa, I'm not hitting earnings because I'm growing so fast on the Internet.'"

It's highly unlikely Best Buy will ever go bankrupt. The comparisons to Circuit City are superficial. Yes, both retailers sold electronics, but Circuit City was much smaller than Best Buy and suffered from a lack of liquidity. The best way to tell if a national retail chain faces doom is when it starts to close a large number of stores.

But both Best Buy and Target stated several times in this book that the store will remain the center of their operations and identity.

"I firmly believe the store has a vital role to play to shopping going forward because it serves a lot of other purposes besides just getting a product at a location," said Target digital chief Casey Carl. "We firmly believe in turning our store into the best not only showroom, but fulfillment center, and also a place for community and commerce to happen. That's really the reason for going forward."

Of course, that doesn't mean the stores will look the same. Both analysts and executives think that big box might be the mall of the future, where the store hosts shops from vendors and perhaps even outside retailers.

"If you read about the history of malls, everything that's sold today between Macy's and Nordstrom in the mall used to be sold in Macy's or Nordstrom, or their predecessor big boxes back in the 1970s," said a top executive at Best Buy. "What's happened over the last several years is that merchandise is moving back into the big boxes. This could be huge for us at Best Buy, being in a big box."

"Some of the underperforming malls aren't going to be here in five years," said retail consultant Keith Anderson. "It's definitely a scenario I think a lot about. That some of the underperforming malls may go into even faster downward spirals than any of the big-box players. If that happens, the big boxes have a huge opportunity to position themselves as right-size, right-location, one-stop shops with maybe slightly more diverse assortments, a bigger emphasis on services as well as just products. That really is sort of where the big-box players are headed."

"They are already taking a huge look at the merchandise they sell," Anderson said. "They're looking at every category and deciding, 'Do we think we can win here and do we think it has a future?' Secondly, they're all investing in services; Best Buy most aggressively with Geek Squad. I think you'll see a lot of movement in services in healthcare and the physical store is going to be a really important environment for that."

Big boxes are also experimenting with smaller formats. Target, for instance, launched an urban format called CityTarget in the downtowns of half of a dozen cities. The company is also testing an even smaller format near the University of Minnesota.

Best Buy has long been testing 50,000-square-foot stores across the country. The company even sells merchandise in airport kiosks.

"I love the Best Buy Express kiosks that you see in the airports," Joly said. "I could see the format populate some large campuses and hotels. We could land quite many more of these in high-traffic places. In many airports you see consumer and electronic specialty stores that are small format. When I was at TGI Fridays we did have restaurants in the airports that were quite comfortable. Why are we not there? It's crazy."

Best Buy and Target also know they need to quickly expand their digital operations to, if anything, generate revenue that will give them more time to transform into true omnichannel retailers.

"Our behaviors as consumers and the way that we interact with retailers and brands is going to be much more greatly tethered together by technology," said retail consultant Doug Stephens. "I think that we're starting to see right now some of the very nascent behaviors that are just going to become more profound over time. You know, I'm having my needs and preferences served up to me in a more efficient and relevant way."

"Retailers have a better sense of what I as an individual prefer, like, and am apt to buy at certain times of the year and [are] serving those recommendations up to me in a much more timely and relevant fashion," he said.

"In ten years, I suspect that we will be, on a daily, weekly basis, ordering a tremendous amount of things that will come to us without the need to go to a store," Stephens said. "I believe that we're probably going to be, most of us, using some sort of dropbox or digital lockbox outside of our homes where things are delivered and you pick them up each day. Big Data, mobile technology, and the pervasiveness of online purchasing are going to be the big changes."

But even in this future, the big box will still form the central core of Best Buy and Target.

"Our stores and our talent will always be our best assets we ever have," Carl said. "If we were building a new Target tomorrow from scratch, we'd still build stores because it's that vital to our strategy. It's a critical piece of our DNA and will be forever. It's what's made Target Target. It's what people know and love about Target."

"Stores have a vital role no matter where guests want to actually transact with us," he said. "Stores are the critical part of their shopping journey with us. They love the experience. It's not a chore. They love coming to Target. It's inspiring. It can be a great outlet if a mom needs a break from her kids. It's a convenience play. It serves all these things in our guests' lives. Stores will be the greatest strategic asset we will ever have."

NOTES

CHAPTER 1: EVERYTHING MUST GO

1. Richard Schulze, *Becoming the Best* (Minneapolis: privately published, 2010), 76–77.
2. Ibid., 32.
3. United States Tariff Commission report, June 1972.
4. Schulze, *Becoming the Best*, 49.
5. Ibid., 52.
6. Ibid., 65.
7. Ibid., 76.
8. Thomas Lee, David Shaffer, Paul McEnroe, "The Lost Empire," *Minneapolis Star Tribune*, November 18, 2012.
9. Schulze, *Becoming the Best*, 78.
10. Ibid., 80.
11. Ibid., 82.

CHAPTER 2: CHEAP CHIC

1. "The Past And Future Of America's Biggest Retailers," NPR.org, November 19, 2012, http://www.npr.org/2012/11/19/165295840/the-past-and-future-of-americas-biggest-retailers.
2. Bruce Dayton, *The Birth of Target* (Minneapolis: privately published, 2008), 24.
3. Ibid., 24.
4. Ibid., 29–43.
5. Ibid., 56.
6. Ibid., 60.
7. Ibid., 60.

8. Ibid., 60.

9. Ibid., 63.

10. Ibid., 63.

11. Ibid., 72.

12. Laura Rowley, *On Target* (New Jersey: John Wiley & Sons Inc., 2003), 20–21.

13. Ibid., 21.

14. Ibid., 21.

15. Thomas Lee, Dave Shaffer, Paul McEnroe, "The Lost Empire," *Minneapolis Star Tribune*, November 18, 2012.

16. Ibid.

17. Alan Wurtzel, *Good to Great to Gone* (New York: Diversion Books, 2012), 215.

CHAPTER 3: THE BURNING PLATFORM

1. Thomas Lee, David Shaffer, and Paul McEnroe, "The Lost Empire," *Minneapolis Star Tribune*, November 18, 2012.

2. Ibid.

3. Ibid.

4. Ibid.

5. Ibid.

6. Ibid.

7. Ibid.

8. Ibid.

9. Ibid.

10. Ibid.

11. Robert Stephens, speech to the North American Conference on Customer Management, November 2003.

12. Ibid.

13. Ibid.

14. Ibid.

15. Ibid.

16. Ibid.

17. Walter Isaacson, *Steve Jobs* (New York: Simon & Schuster, 2011), 376.

18. Thomas Lee, "Best Buy Stakes a Huge Part of Its Future on Geek Squad," *Minneapolis Star Tribune*, July 29, 2012.

19. Lee, Shaffer, and McEnroe, "The Lost Empire."

20. Ranjay Gulati, "Inside Best Buy's Customer-Centric Strategy," *Harvard Business Review*, April 12, 2010.

21. Ibid.

22. Ibid.

CHAPTER 4: "I HOPE I WAKE UP SMARTER"

1. Thomas Lee, David Shaffer, and Paul McEnroe, "The Lost Empire," *Minneapolis Star Tribune*, November 18, 2012.

2. Ranjay Gulati, "Inside Best Buy's Customer-Centric Strategy," *Harvard Business Review*, April 12, 2010.

3. Lee, Shaffer, and McEnroe, "The Lost Empire."

4. Tony Kennedy, Paul McEnroe, Patrick Kennedy, Thomas Lee, and Eric Wieffering, "Brian Dunn: The Rise and Fall of a Salesman," *Minneapolis Star Tribune*, April 22, 2012.

5. "Best Buy Founder Richard Schulze Sends Letter to Board Affirming Commitment to Acquisition," BusinessWire.com, August 16, 2012, http://www.businesswire.com/news/home/20120816005565/en/Buy-Founder-Richard-Schulze-Sends-Letter-Board#.U5uUvnb-Rx0.

6. Lee, Shaffer, and McEnroe, "The Lost Empire."

7. Ibid.

8. Kantar Retail, "The Target Shopper," September 26, 2013.

9. Ibid.

10. Walter Isaacson, *Steve Jobs* (New York: Simon & Schuster, 2011), 389.

11. Thomas Lee, "Web Wars: Target.com vs. Walmart.com," *Minneapolis Star Tribune*, December 5, 2007.

12. "comScore Reports $186.2 Billion in Full Year 2012 U.S. Retail E-Commerce Spending, Up 15 Percent vs. Year Ago," press release, comScore, February 7, 2013, http://www.comscore.com/Insights/Press-Releases/2013/2/comScore-Reports-186.2-Billion-in-Full-Year-2012-U.S.-Retail-E-Commerce-Spending.

13. "Gartner Says Declining Worldwide PC Shipments in Fourth Quarter of 2012 Signal Structural Shift of PC Market," press release, Gartner, January 14, 2013, http://www.gartner.com/newsroom/id/2301715.

14. "U.S. Shipment Numbers, 2008–2009," RIAA, https://www.riaa.com/key-statistics.php?content_selector=2008–2009-U.S-Shipment-Numbers.

15. Kantar Retail, "The Target Shopper."

16. ShopperTrak, "Best Practices for Implementing In-Store Analytics in Bricks and Mortar Retail," White paper, http://www.shoppertrak.com/resources/whitepapers/best-practices-implementing-store-analytics-bricks-mortar-retail/.

17. Thomas Lee, "Best Buy's New Chief Is Selling from Day 1," *Minneapolis Star Tribune*, September 9, 2012.

18. Thomas Lee, "Best Buy Standoff Evolved into Schulze-Joly Alliance," *Minneapolis Star Tribune*, March 26, 2013.

19. Ibid.

20. Ibid.

21. Ibid.

CHAPTER 5: WALK BEFORE YOU CAN RUN

1. Hubert Joly, Best Buy sales conference, October 15, 2013.

2. Ibid.

3. Ibid.

4. Ibid.

5. Professor Claes Fornell, "ACSI Retail and E-Commerce Report 2012," American Customer Satisfaction Index, February 26, 2013, http://www.theacsi.org/news-and-resources/customer-satisfaction-reports/customer-satisfaction-reports-2012/acsi-retail-and-e-commerce-report-2012.

6. Joly, Best Buy sales conference.

7. Ibid.

8. Ibid.

9. Kantar Retail, "The Target Shopper," September 26, 2013.

CHAPTER 6: ROOM TO ROAM

1. Thomas Lee, "Best Buy and Samsung Further Tie the Knot," *Minneapolis Star Tribune*, April 21, 2013.

2. Ibid.

3. Kinshuk Jerath and Z. John Zhang, "Store-Within-a-Store," *Journal of Marketing Research*, June 2009, http://www.andrew.cmu.edu/user/kinshuk/cvdocs/JZ_SnS.pdf.

4. "Sony Electronics to Launch New Retail Space, 'Sony Experience at Best Buy,' in approximately 350 Stores Nationwide," press release, Sony, May

1, 2014, http://www.sony.com/SCA/company-news/press-releases/sony-electronics/2014/sony-electronics-to-launch-new-retail-space-sony-e.shtml.

5. Ibid.

6. Sharon McCollam, Goldman Sachs dotCommerce conference, June 6, 2013.

7. Ibid.

8. Curtis Greve and Jerry Davis, "Recovering Lost Profits by Improving Reverse Logistics," http://www.ups.com/media/en/Reverse_Logistics_wp.pdf.

9. McCollam, Goldman Sachs dotCommerce conference.

10. Thomas Lee, "Best Buy Uses Geek Squad to Get More for Its Returns," *Minneapolis Star Tribune*, January 19, 2014.

11. "Best Buy's Showrooming Strategy Resonating with Mobile Shoppers," Prosper Insights and Analytics, June 26, 2013, http://prosperdiscovery.com/best-buys-showrooming-strategy-resonating-with-mobile-shoppers/.

12. "Mobile Influence 2013," Deloitte Digital, http://www2.deloitte.com/content/dam/Deloitte/ie/Documents/ConsumerBusiness/2013_mobile_influence_deloitte_ireland.pdf.

13. "Best Buy's Showrooming Strategy Resonating with Mobile Shoppers."

14. Kantar Retail, "The Target Shopper," September 26, 2013.

CHAPTER 7: "FIRE A LOT OF BULLETS"

1. Thomas Lee, "Holiday Shoppers Embrace E-Commerce," *Minneapolis Star Tribune,* December 10, 2011.

2. Bruce Dayton, *The Birth of Target* (Minneapolis: privately published, 2008), 54.

3. Ibid., 83–84.

4. Thomas Lee, "Target Corp. Eyes Silicon Valley with Innovation Center in San Francisco," *Minneapolis Star Tribune*, August 5, 2013. Beth Jacob no longer works at Target. She was fired after the hackers stole personal data from over 100 million customers at Target in December 2013.

5. Thomas Lee, "Best Buy's New Chief Is Selling From Day 1," *Minneapolis Star Tribune*, September 8, 2012.

6. Hubert Joly, Best Buy sales conference, October 15, 2013.

7. Robin Lewis, "How Best Buy Blew the Chance to Out-Apple Apple," *The Robin Report*, http://therobinreport.com/how-best-buy-blew-the-chance-to-out-apple-apple/.

8. Hubert Joly, "Best Buy CEO on Leadership: A Comment I Made Was Misconstrued," *Minneapolis Star Tribune*, March 17, 2013.

9. Ibid.

CHAPTER 8: JUMBOTRON

1. "Research Shows $14.80 Billion Spent On Video Game Content In The U.S. For 2012," press release, NPD Group, February 6, 2013, https://www.npd.com/wps/portal/npd/us/news/press-releases/research-shows-14.80-billion-spent-on-video-game-content-in-the-us-for-2012/.

2. Thomas Lee, "Target Unveils Exclusive Natori Lingerie Line," *Minneapolis Star Tribune*, October 29, 2011.

3. Thomas Lee, "Target Entertainment Chief: CDs Are Not Dead. Just Ask Taylor Swift," *Minneapolis Star* Tribune, October 21, 2011.

4. Thomas Lee, "One Year Into the Job, Target Marketing Chief Already Leaves Mark," *Minneapolis Star Tribune*, April 28, 2013.

5. Kantar Retail, "Target Today: Focus on Brick & Mortar," September 25, 2013.

6. Kantar Retail, "The Target Shopper," September 26, 2013.

7. Kantar Retail, "Target Today."

CHAPTER 9: VALENTINE'S DAY SURPRISE

1. "IndoorAtlas Introduces Industry's First Geomagnetic-Based Indoor Mapping App for iOS," MarketWired, April 24, 2014, http://www.marketwired.com/press-release/indooratlas-introduces-industrys-first-geomagnetic-based-indoor-mapping-app-for-ios-1902786.htm.

2. "New Privacy Study Finds 79 Percent of Customers are Willing to Provide Personal Information to a 'Trusted Brand'," SDL, January 26, 2014, http://www.sdl.com/aboutus/news/pressreleases/2014/new-privacy-study-finds-79-percent-of-customers-are-willing-to-provide-personal-information-to-a-trusted-brand.html.

3. Jeff Fromm, Celeste Lindell, and Lainie Decker, "American Millennials: Deciphering the Enigma Generation," Barkley, 2011, http://barkley.s3.amazonaws.com/barkleyus/AmericanMillennials.pdf.

4. Ibid.

5. "Target Corporation's CEO Discusses Q4 2013 Results—Earnings Call Transcript," Seeking Alpha, February 26, 2014, http://seekingalpha.com

/article/2051063-target-corporations-ceo-discusses-q4–2013-results-earnings-call-transcript.

6. Fromm, Lindell, and Decke, "American Millennials."

7. Greg Buzek, "Why Charity in Retail Is Good Business," IHL Services, April 19, 2011, http://www.ihlservices.com/ihl/product_detail.cfm?page=Marketing%20and%20Operations&ProductID=70.

8. Thomas Lee, "Target Partners with Niece of Former President George W. Bush," *Minneapolis Star Tribune*, March 12, 2013.

9. Ibid.

10. Mike Schneider, "Half of top US internet retailers still failing to deliver real social customer service," Conversocial, July 17, 2013, http://www.conversocial.com/blog/half-of-top-us-internet-retailers-still-failing-to-deliver-real-social-customer-service#.U97fl6P-Rx0.

11. Thomas Lee, "With Shoppable Hangout, Best Buy Marries Social Media to Commerce," *Minneapolis Star Tribune*, December 25, 2013.

CONCLUSION: BIG IS BETTER

1. Hubert Joly, Best Buy sales conference, October 15, 2013.

2. Thomas Lee, "Best Buy CEO Hubert Joly Is Unshaken by 29% Stock Plunge," *Minneapolis Star Tribune*, January 17, 2014.

BIBLIOGRAPHY

BOOKS

Dayton, Bruce. *The Birth of Target*. Minneapolis: privately published, 2008.

Isaacson, Walter. *Steve Jobs*. New York: Simon & Schuster, 2013.

Rowley, Laura. *On Target*. New York: John Wiley & Sons, 2003.

Schulze, Richard M. *Becoming the Best*. Minneapolis: privately published, 2010.

Wurtzel, Alan. *Good to Great to Gone*. New York: Diversion Books, 2012.

MAGAZINES

Ranjay Gulati, "Inside Best Buy's Customer-Centric Strategy," Harvard Business Review, April 12, 2010.

NEWSPAPERS

Joly, Hubert. "Best Buy CEO on Leadership: A Comment I Made Was Misconstrued." *Minneapolis Star Tribune,* March 17, 2013.

Kennedy, Tony, Paul McEnroe, Patrick Kennedy, Thomas Lee, Eric Wieffering. "Brian Dunn: The Rise and Fall of a Salesman." *Minneapolis Star Tribune,* April 22, 2012.

Lee, Thomas. "Best Buy and Samsung Further Tie the Knot." *Minneapolis Star Tribune*, April 21, 2013.

———. "Best Buy's New Chief Is Selling from Day 1." *Minneapolis Star Tribune,* September 9, 2012.

———. "Best Buy Stakes a Huge Part of Its Future on Geek Squad." *Minneapolis Star Tribune*, July 29, 2012.

————. "Best Buy Standoff Evolved into Schulze-Joly Alliance." *Minneapolis Star Tribune*, March 26, 2013.

————. "Best Buy Uses Geek Squad to Get More on Its Returns." Minneapolis Star Tribune, January 19, 2014.

————. "Holiday Shoppers Embrace E-commerce." *Minneapolis Star Tribune*, December 10, 2011.

————. "One Year into the Job, Target Marketing Chief Already Leaves Mark." *Minneapolis Star Tribune*, April 28, 2013.

————. "Target Corp. Eyes Silicon Valley with Innovation Center in San Francisco." *Minneapolis Star Tribune*, August 5, 2013.

————. "Target Entertainment Chief: CDs Are Not Dead. Just Ask Taylor Swift." *Minneapolis Star Tribune*, October 21, 2011.

————. "Target Partners with Niece of Former President George W. Bush." *Minneapolis Star Tribune*, March 12, 2013.

————. "Target Unveils Exclusive Natori Lingerie Line." *Minneapolis Star Tribune*, October 29, 2011.

————. "Web Wars: Target.com vs. Walmart.com." *Minneapolis Star Tribune*, December 5, 2007.

————. "With Shoppable Hangout, Best Buy Marries Social Media to Commerce," *Minneapolis Star Tribune*, December 25, 2013.

Lee, Thomas, David Shaffer, Paul McEnroe. "The Lost Empire." *Minneapolis Star Tribune*, November 18, 2012.

INDEX